The Ottakar's LOCAL HISTORY *Series*

Darlington

Mrs Minnie Mudd with son ernest.

Ottakar's LOCAL HISTORY *Series*

Darlington

Compiled by
Claire Bulman

OTTAKAR'S

TEMPUS

First published 2001
Copyright © Ottakar's plc, 2001

Ottakar's Local History Series
produced in association with
Tempus Publishing Limited
The Mill, Brimscombe Port,
Stroud, Gloucestershire, GL5 2QG

ISBN 0 7524 2286 3

Typesetting and origination by
Tempus Publishing Limited
Printed in Great Britain by
Midway Colour Print, Wiltshire

Party in Brunswick Street to celebrate the end of the war. (Copyright, The Northern Echo)

Contents

Foreword

It was with some excitement that Ottakar's started out on a venture that became known as the Local History Project, an attempt to uncover the past in Darlington from a variety of viewpoints.

The Local History Project asked people to send in articles – either their own memories or researched pieces of local history – with the best ones being published in this book. I was massively encouraged by the response, both in terms of the quality and the passion with which people participated. I believe that we have been able to create a unique document, chronicling Darlington in a way that has never been done before.

Included in this collection are recollections of many aspects of life in Darlington, including childhood, local residents, buildings and landmarks, the railways and industry, sport and pastimes and the history of some of the surrounding villages and towns.

What has become obvious in editing this book is that Darlington is an area rich in local history. From the formally researched history of St Andrew's church, to the wonderfully anecdotal memories of Joan Bell in *Childhood Traumas*, these are the bedrock of the past that makes Darlington what it is today.

In the Acknowledgements (p. 128) I have thanked many individuals by name. Here I would like to add my general thanks to everyone who has showed an interest in this project. It has been a pleasure to put this book together, and often the hardest decision has been to decide what must be left out. I hope you get as much pleasure in discovering the past in *Darlington*.

Claire Bulman
August 2001

Boat house and bandstand, North Lodge Park.

Introduction

Darlington Remembered

I came to live in Darlington in 1959 and have fond memories of the town before the changes of the 1960s onward, gathered pace. Why come to Darlington? Pretty well all I knew about the north east of England was that there was an early railway, the Stockton and Darlington of course, a Durham coalfield and a waterfall called the High Force on the river Tees.

The reason for leaving Manchester was that my husband's new job was to be centred on Teesside. The firm offered a conducted tour of possible housing. On arriving at Thornaby Station we were dismayed to think that we had to move from Old Trafford, near the Manchester Ship Canal and one of the country's largest concentrations of heavy industry, to a similar smog-shrouded district around the Tees estuary. Out of the frying pan into the fire?

So we made several exploratory visits. New estates were growing near Redcar, Marske and Saltburn, but there was not a tree in sight along the coast and hedges were bent landwards by the wind. A lady in Saltburn told us that her washing would blow dry even when it was raining!

We decided to explore Darlington. Approaching the town along the A1 we could see new houses being built on high ground across the Tees at what proved to be Blackwell and Skerne Park. We turned on to Carmel Road South and were encouraged to see that the houses were painted white or cream instead of the dark serviceable colours of Lancashire and the West Riding. There was also a promise of roses and flowers galore in the front gardens.

Somehow we found ourselves down a narrow lane off Carmel Road North from which new house building could be seen in progress. Three new occupants invited us in, making a welcoming early impression. Hemmed in by the high walls of West Cemetery on one side and Hummersknott parkland on the other, we had to manoeuvre our car out again in the dark. That park wall was later reduced to its foundations. Bussey and Armstrong, Blacketts and Raine Brothers were building on what had been the largest of the Quaker landscaped parks, that of Arthur Pease. Reuban Raine had just the four-bedroomed house we needed, nearing completion but not yet spoken for!

Edinburgh Drive was then only single-tracked as far as the new girls' high school building which HRH The Duke of Edinburgh had ceremonially opened in 1955. For some years until the Peter Plan and comprehensive education, 600 uniformed girls walked quietly along to homes or buses. The local farmer's tractor and muck-spreader passed regularly to reach his remaining fields. Cows grazed and drank at a trough opposite the school.

So one June day in 1959 saw us, our two boys, one grandpa and a tabby cat decamp from a Ford Prefect, having spent our first night in Darlington at Blackwell Hall Hotel, now demolished. That year saw a prolonged heat wave and drought, and builders' rubble and clay soil, like concrete, made hard work of creating a garden.

Cold winters were a feature of our early years, and snow-clearing was a regular chore in town and suburbs. In 1962-63 the Tees was frozen over at Broken Scar dam. On Stainmore, snow-blowing machines sent white fountains into the air as they tried to clear the A66. The High

The new house in Darlington.

Force was like a bridal veil, and its plunge pool froze hard enough for our boys and others to slide on. Aysgarth Falls were like a tiered wedding cake. At the sudden overnight thaw on 5/6 March, ice floes raced along the swollen Tees and smashed ominous and resounding against the piers of Croft Bridge.

Mowden hall parkland was soon to be sold to Yuills for house building and the Edinburgh Drive-Fulthorpe Avenue connection made. The Model T and The Mowden pubs ended the Quaker temperance era.

Settling in meant joining in. Darlington and Teesdale Naturalists' Field Club, founded in 1891, was the nearest in interests for a geographer, and it helped me to get to know the area. We met in a building in the grounds of the Friends Meeting House in Skinnergate. The room was surrounded by solid Victorian display cases, cupboards, specimen drawers and map cases all crammed with wonderful exhibits. On Tuesday evenings we sat on hard wooden benches for lectures and business. Overhead Joy Beadell's dancing class thumped the ceiling. A full programme of summer outings was held, and still is. The club supported the campaign against the spraying of toxic chemicals on roadside verges and supported a campaign against building the Cow Green reservoir, which it was feared would affect the microclimate and put at risk the world-famous surviving Arctic-Alpine flora. Dr Margaret Bradshaw of Durham University voiced the protests and organized a rescue of rare plant assemblages about to be flooded. During the building work, Tom Buffey, the public relations officer was generous in guiding the club on-site visits. Dr David Bellamy the conservationist and TV personality has long been a friend to the club. For our centenary celebrations he led a nostalgic visit to Cow Green, the dam, the flora, the junipers and the ferns of the High Force gorge. Afterwards I was able to answer an appeal to fill a gap in his own collections with a wooden New Zealand butter box stamped with a large fern motif. It had carried some of my books from Manchester to Darlington!

There were moves afoot in 1960, backed by the Mayor, Cllr Watsam Cottam, to form a Darlington Historical Society. This was inaugurated by Cllr Nellie Cottam at a ceremony in the council chamber of the old town hall. There was a fine semi-circle of seats and mayoral bench of Victorian solidity. What happened to them when the new town hall was opened by HRH The Princess Anne in 1970? For the Golden Jubilee of the County Borough of Darlington in 1965, members wrote a booklet *Darlington 50 Years Ago*. In 1967, celebrations marking the centenary of the Charter of Incorporation of Darlington as a Municipal Borough granted by Her Majesty Queen Victoria included an exhibition in Kendrew Street Baths Hall in which the Historical Society created an ornate Victorian drawing room. The grand celebrations were marked by a visit of Her Majesty Queen Elizabeth II and HRH The Duke of Edinburgh. A leather-bound copy of our chairman Norman Sunderland's *A History of Darlington*, published by the society for the centenary and helped by a grant from the borough council, was presented to Her Majesty. However, in 1974 Darlington became a District under Durham County Council but in 1997 regained its Unitary status.

The Historical Society also backed Norman Sunderland in an attempt to save the only Tudor building to survive the Great Fire of Darlington in 1585, which had destroyed 273 buildings in the town centre. The Nag's Head public house in Tubwell Row had once been St Cuthbert's vicarage. In the event, the patterned brick rear wall was preserved, is now a Listed Building, and can be seen in Church Lane. The Society's requests to retrieve the old market cross, however, were less successful. Situated at the top of Tubwell Row until the town clock tower was built, then inside the covered Market Hall and latterly languishing in Hundens Council Yard it has now been restored and sited at the top end of Market Place during the 1990s refurbishment.

Meanwhile, the old town hall had long been inadequate for the growing town. In 1901 the council bought North Lodge mansion in Northgate for council offices and proposed to build a new wing for a council chamber, committee rooms and a museum. In 1930 there were moves to build a new town hall on two acres behind North Lodge Park Bowling Green. By the 1960s, however, the borough council's offices were scattered around the town. The Education Department was in North Lodge villa, the Architect's Department at Bennet House, The Transport Department and the Town Clerks Department were in Houndgate, the Registry Department in East Street and one paid one's rates over a mahogany counter at Central Hall in Bull Wynd. The town clerk used to relate that he could walk on a rainy day from his Houndgate office to Northgate without getting wet, taking a route through Central Hall, the Architect's offices, the covered market or under its glass canopy, through the Co-op from

The covered market before refurbishment, December 1973. (Vera Chapman)

Tubwell Row to Priestgate and thence through Woolworth's rear to Northgate!

Somewhat later, the Edwardian Hippodrome and Palace of Varieties in Parkgate, built for 1,210 in 1907 and owned and preserved by Darlington Operatic Society, was transformed by the borough council into Darlington Civic Theatre to seat a more realistic 601. This left space to create a theatre lounge bar, where the Friends of the Civic, founded in 1965 and abetted by the energetic young theatre director Peter Todd, could welcome and entertain visiting actors. The Friends also helped to fund behind the scenes amenities for the actors. Cassy Harker, the retired matron of Darlington Memorial Hospital, was our chairman and we organized visits to other theatres in the region. A Circle Bar was later built, during which time the remains were found of the pet dog of Monsieur Pepi, the first director. Maybe the ghosts of both have now been laid to rest!

To return to our early days, however, grandpa found it difficult to settle in a new place and make friends. However, an over-sixties type club was opened in Salutation Road church hall and flourished, managing its own affairs and even running holiday tours. So grandpa made new friends and was introduced to the Conservative Association Social Club in Russell Street, formerly the town's first cottage hospital and dispensary.

Another circumstance also helped him. Patons and Baldwins had set up their new knitting yarns factory in Darlington at McMullen Road. Many of their Halifax workers had come too. So grandpa, long a Halifax man, found near neighbours and to his surprise a cousin with whom he could share common ground. Also, being a former amateur cricketer, he was wont to remark on entering Darlington that the sight of the three chimneys of the town's electric power station, which he nicknamed 'the wickets', made him feel at home!

The cat, however, was a different matter. Originally a stray that had adopted us, his transfer to a house in Darlington was not to his liking and he scarpered after three days!

The boys settled more easily. Neighbouring children came round and there was soon school for them to make new friends. There was Miss Herriman at Abbey Road and Dr Hare at the grammar school. Cubs did not attract, but train spotting was compulsive. It was a gift at Bank Top main-line station, the roundhouse engine shed and the pedestrian bridge. Adding to this was the excitement of the early 1960s during the Beeching closures, chasing final journeys and riding behind a J21 over Stainmore summit.

But Darlington's function as a railway-manufacturing town was soon to be wiped out. North Road shops, the town's largest works was then still building, repairing and overhauling steam engines. At its peak, around 3,500 men were employed there, which one could well believe as they came pouring out on bicycles at the end of shifts. Irene Smith's bicycle shop across North Road flourished until the works closed.

There was also Robert Stephenson and Hawthorn's Springfield Works making diesel and electric locomotives, Stooperdale Boiler Shops and Faverdale Waggon Works. The heavy iron industries established in the nineteenth century were also at work: Summerson's Foundries,

New recruits at Patons & Baldwins, 1961.

Patons & Baldwins Factory. (Copyright, The Northern Echo)

Darlington Forge and Darlington and Simpson Rolling Mills. Alongside the main line were Cleveland Bridge and Engineering Company and W. Richardson and Company, heating engineers who made greenhouses, conservatories and industrial heating systems. Their tall thermometer was a landmark for railway travellers coming northward.

All of these closed down, as did Pease's Mill, Paton's factory and Alexander's. About 10,000 jobs were lost, yet it was exciting to see new firms set up at Yarm Road as Darlington diversified. The polished steel sculpture 'Resurgence' on the new Town Hall forecourt of 1970 celebrates past achievements and future prosperity.

The town centre shops were still mainly family businesses or branches of local origin. On High Row were Binns, John Grizedale, Liptons, Lucks, Backhouse's Bank, and Dressers; in Post House Wynd Isabel Moore, Hoppers Jewellers, Simpson's Sports, Browns printers; on Blackwellgate the SPCK bookshop and The Fleece Hotel; on Northgate Doggarts and Cox and Falkoner; on Bondgate Moses furniture; on Horsemarket John Lear and Sons ironmongery and on Bakehouse Hill Thomas Pease and Co., grocery, wines and spirits. Skinnergate had Bainbridge Barker's department store, but perhaps most memorably were the enticing smells from Zizzler the pork butcher's, Wildsmith's cheese, bacon and coffee, and there was Pressland's the hairdresser whose perfumes wafted out along the street. On Teesside, a 'gentleman' was defined as one who came to Darlington to have his hair cut!

The covered market also housed local small businesses (and still does) like Murray the Baker, Harrison butchers and Sandersons greengrocery.

In the 1960s a few people still lived in houses in some of the old yards, for example, Russell Yard off High Row and Potter's Yard off Bondgate and were reluctant to be moved. Three yards still house small businesses.

The outdoor market stalls had grey canopies, and frames were stored on the corner of Feethams, whilst the Square was most of the time a car park. A proposal to build an Arndale Shopping Centre over much of the market square was repudiated. The outdoor bus station was down the Lead Yard, next to St Cuthbert's church, which was obscured by mature trees and evergreen shrubs in its long-closed graveyard.

Traffic queued on Grange Road to get through the town centre, which was a part of the

Harrison's Butchers in the covered market, 1932. The family business was established in 1799 in Park Street.

HOUNDGATE, DARLINGTON — OLD WAREHOUSES and PEASE'S HOUSE.

Above: *Old warehouses and Pease's House in Houndgate. (Vera Chapman).*
Below: *Old Darlington, Slater's Yard, Bondgate. (Vera Chapman).*

historic Great North Road. There was delay at a Belisha beacon crossing. Relief was needed. So in 1965 came the Darlington bypass and then, in stages, the Inner Ring Road. But that introduces another and later story of change and improvement. Yet Darlington has retained much of its historic character and charm, and has been voted by the Civic Trust as one of the best six towns in which to live and work.

Vera Chapman
August 2001

CHAPTER 1
Childhood

John Brown's Saw Mills, John Street. Timber wagons are seen here bringing locally-felled trees into the timber yard around 1900-1920. (Copyright, Centre for Local Studies, Darlington Library)

The Coal Shortage

In 1926 we had the National Coal Strike and, more than ever before, we had to rely on coke (or cinders as we called them) to do the household chores of cooking, heating and washing. In the living room there was the old-fashioned, black leaded iron range, with the oven on the left hand side. There was an open grating for a fire in the centre. At the right hand side of the fire was a small boiler, which, having been filled with cold water from the back kitchen tap, used to provide a modicum of hot water if the fire was on, or had been on recently.

One day, with our fuel situation desperate, my father got my elder brother and I together, saying that we had to go to bed early because he would wake us at about 4.00 a.m. It would be quite dark but we were to take our bogie and go to the local gas works in John Street, where we would join the queue to await the opening of the gates at 7.30 a.m. We would then be able to buy tickets for 1cwt of cinders, which would fill the bogie.

It was dark, but cold and dry, when father helped us to manhandle the bogie out of the back door and into the back lane. We made our way slowly, hoping that the clatter from the iron wheels didn't awaken the neighbourhood. The streets at that time of night were silent and empty, and we couldn't drown the rumbling noise from our bogie.

It was quite a walk through the streets lit only by an occasional gas lamp. We headed first along Bedford Street and into Backhouse Street and then into Parkgate. Eventually we reached our destination of John Street with Brown's Sawmills on one side and the gas works, with its towering gasholders, on the other side.

Even at that time there was a queue of people, huddling together, to keep the cold from numbing their bones. We joined the queue, leaving our bogie close by in the gutter. My brother and I took turns to leave our place and hastily climb into the bogie, trying to escape, even for a minute or two, the cold bitterness of the searching icy wind.

I had noticed, shortly after joining the queue, a policeman who was on a sort of slow patrol further down the road. He singled out two little boys, who after being spoken to by the constable, had slowly walked away into the darkness. The man seemed to be searching amongst the queue and he was heading in our direction. Finally, he arrived and on seeing us two boys, came up to us, wanting to know our names and where we lived. 'You shouldn't be here, neither of you. You should be back home in bed. So come on, lets have you,' he said, shining his lamp into our faces. We simply could not return home empty handed, we just had to get some cinders. Then the unexpected occurred, a man in the queue stepped forward. 'What's the matter, officer? They aren't causing any trouble. Why can't you leave them alone? Of course, they would like to be at home in their beds – so would we, so would everybody, and perhaps, so would you. Leave them here, they deserve their place in the queue.' Then he paused, looked the officer straight in the face, and said, 'If there's going to be any trouble here, you may cause it.' At this point it looked like a bit of a 'stand-off'. The people nearby in the queue spoke up in protest at the officer's attitude. Eventually, he backed off, mumbled a few remarks and walked away. Perhaps if he hadn't been on his own, things might have turned out differently.

As time passed the residents of John Street emerged from their dingy terraced houses carrying sustenance in the form of hot tea, slices of bread and jam and biscuits. They handed the food to people in the queue. This was a truly generous gesture by sympathetic neighbours and the memory of this incident still lingers with me.

At 7.30 a.m. prompt the works' gates opened and the long-suffering members of the queue moved slowly forward to the office, where they were issued with tickets. Pushing their wheeled wooden 'vehicles' they finally arrived at the place where their requirements were met by a wizened old man. He wielded his large fork into the large pile of cinders, enabling him to throw the fork's loaded contents into whatever receptacle was placed before him. I can still see him as he carried out his work, not saying a word to anyone, chewing away at whatever it was, but when he occasionally spat out it produced quite a dark stain on the cobblestones. Finally, we gave him the appropriate ticket, which he in turn inserted into a slot in a box attached to his weighing scales.

Of course, with the passing of time, I returned to the gas works many times. Eventually, however, the old man of the scales was 'absent' and so was the dark stain on the cobblestones.

W.G. Ellis

Schooldays

In 1954 when I was a shy five-year-old girl I started school. The Holy Family Primary School in Prior Street, Cockerton was a small grey-bricked building. Outside was a draughty playground and dour, dank toilets that invariably froze over in winter.

Inside, crates of free school milk were stacked in the corridor and bottles were handed out daily to all the pupils, chunks of ice floated in it in winter while in summer it tasted warm and slightly rancid. In class we recited, in a parrot fashion, our multiplication tables and our catechism.

The cane was an integral part of school life; I received it only once for the minor misdemeanor of copying the word grammar incorrectly from the blackboard. Classes were mixed and games or PE, often in the guise of team games, was competitive; both sexes were taught country dancing and we entered the music festival held at Eastbourne School each year and were successful several times.

At playtime the boys innocently played imaginary games of Cowboys and Indians or cops and robbers, often taking some unsuspecting, yet secretly delighted girl, prisoner and threatening to scalp or murder her. The times of political correctness were still unheard of. Skipping games were popular and often teachers joined in the fun. The hula hoop was fashionable then.

Before, and after school we used to run eagerly to Miss Wheel's sweet shop-cum-terraced house, halfway down Prior Street. From behind a wooden counter in her front room, she sold enormous bright red gobstoppers, black liquorice sticks and shiny yellow and red fruit salad chews for one old penny.

The modern Catholic church now visible from Cockerton Green was not built in 1954 and the original church was attached to the school, which is now the social centre. Outside the school was an immaculate lawn surrounded by trees. Back in the fifties the lawn was used for the yearly religious processions held on feast days and the boys, faces scrubbed and shiny, dressed in starched white shirts, red ties and short grey trousers, joined the girls who wore pristine white dresses and veils for the occasion. In the fifties primary school education was geared to what seemed to be the equivalent of finding the holy grail – passing the eleven-plus and gaining a place at one of the local Catholic grammar schools. For the girls the grammar school was The Immaculate Conception also known as Southend (formerly the home of Joseph Pease whose statue stands on High Row). For the boys passing the eleven-plus meant a place at St

Mary's which, when comprehensive education was introduced, became Carmel Comprehensive and is now Carmel Technology College.

In our final year at primary school everyone sat the eleven-plus. Brown envelopes brought the long awaited results (which in those days probably mapped out your future). I passed and a place at the Immaculate Conception was mine. My delighted parents presented me with a second-hand blue and white bike and a Kodak camera that took tiny black and white photographs.

Doggart's department store on Northgate sold the prestigious uniform of blue beret and blazer, a navy pleated skirt that covered the knees, yellow and blue striped tie and shiny brown satchel. I remember the strange system of payment as the money was pushed into small metal cylinders and the lids firmly closed. The cylinders then whizzed silently along taut thin wires to an unseen but obviously superior being who dealt with the payments.

After wonderful carefree days at my tiny primary school I found the cloistered blue stocking world of an all girls convent difficult to adjust to. Here pupils included scholarship girls from the surrounding area, fee-paying daygirls and boarders. One day a boarder reduced us all to green-eyed envy when she showed us a diamond she said had been sent from her parents in South Africa as a birthday present.

The convent was formerly Joseph Pease's mansion, standing on the corner of Southend Avenue and Coniscliffe Road, (it is now the Grange Hotel). It also had a modern annexe attached, which contained some classrooms, a sports hall and a kindergarten. This was demolished when the school closed and is now the site of Westcliffe Court.

The sports hall doubled as an assembly hall where morning prayers were said every day. In summer the heat in the crowded hall was suffocating and fainting was commonplace. From the windows of the classrooms there were wonderful views of the extensive grounds. St Augustine's primary school is now located in this area. In the main body of the convent narrow stone staircases led to more classrooms while downstairs cool airy corridors did the same. Also there was a small chapel where we went on retreat, days of prayer and silence. The Sisters of Charity or female teachers, wearing flowing black gowns and mortarboards, taught us a variety of subjects including French and Latin, again partly taught parrot fashion. There were also lessons in maths, science and religious education but not cookery for some inexplicable reason. (It was whispered that the sisters, who to us seemed to be trapped in a time warp, thought we would marry wealthy men who would provide us with domestic staff.)

As at primary school, on feast days processions were held in the landscaped grounds and we knelt on the gravel paths, again dressed in white dresses and veils, on pebbles which dug into our bare knees leaving red welts and large indentations. Outside the convent it was the swinging sixties and in those days most girls smuggled posters of the Beatles or Rolling Stones into school! After school a favourite place to hang out was a coffee bar in Post House Wynd called Dipalo's I think.

We all received an excellent education, however, and we respected our teachers. In the sixties career choices appeared limited and probably the most popular profession for girls, unlike today, was teaching and many girls went on to teacher-training college.

Carol Middleton

Childhood Traumas

In 1932 my mother launched me into this world a hefty 10lbs. Poor mam. No gas and air just sheer brute force. When mam found herself pregnant again six months later she was determined not to repeat the experience. A friend told her to take Epsom salts every day. The same midwife attended the birth of my brother who weighed in at just 6lbs. The midwife commented on the difference in birth weights and was aghast when she heard the explanation. She told my mother that my brother could have died. Such was the ignorance on medical matters then.

The consequences of this were long lasting. My brother was considered delicate and it was difficult to put weight on him. The doctor gave mam a note to buy goats milk for him, which was provided by a man who kept goats on Eastbourne allotments. This continued through the war years. When he started school he was taken every week to the school clinic, at Greenbank, for sunray treatment. During the war he was sent to stay at Peat's Home. Cllr Peat opened his home to children who needed special care. They spent two weeks being 'built up' with fresh farm produce and fresh country air. I cannot remember Cllr Peat's generosity being acknowledged. Though my brother appeared delicate and slightly smaller in stature to his siblings, he grew into a strong wiry youth.

My own, first experience of the 'school clinic' was the dentist, a dreadful man. I arrived at the school clinic with my mother filled with apprehension. As we sat on the benches in that large waiting room I watched the children on their return walking past to the exit, some in floods of tears. My apprehension was mounting to a feeling of terror. This was heightened when the dentist strapped me into the chair with a broad leather belt. I responded to 'open wide' and he used his fingers to keep my jaw open. I did not mean to bite his fingers but I was completely unprepared for the needle he jabbed into my gum and I succumbed to the reflex action and snapped my teeth together. He was unprepared too because his fingers were still in my mouth. He was furious and refused to take the tooth out.

I then had to listen to the tirade of my mother and it did not end there. Next morning after register at school Miss Connelly said, 'Stand up Joan Parkes.' She then addressed the class. 'Do you know what Joan Parkes did? She bit the dentist's finger. Wasn't she a bad girl?' There were nods and murmurs of assent from the class. Then she turned to me. 'Sit down you bad girl.' So there I sat, five years old close to tears, drowning in humiliation, trying to concentrate on chanting the Catechism. Ever after visits to the dentist were always a traumatic experience.

Joan Bell

Bondgate Revisited

I was born in 1936 at No. 2 Slater's Buildings, Bondgate and lived there until the age of eighteen. Looking back I realize that, although we had no bathroom or electricity and therefore none of the luxuries that most people took for granted, there was a real sense of community, which

Bondgate, 1920s. (Copyright, The Northern Echo)

does not exist today. People really did borrow a cup of sugar or an egg until payday.

There were five houses in the main yard together with a row of toilets and coalhouses. There was also a communal washhouse complete with a large boiler. As a result washday meant exactly that! It was a whole day of washing, possing, boiling and wringing. (Oh, how I love my automatic washer!)

Slater's Buildings were separated from Trenholme Terrace by a 6ft wall. There were about five houses that had tiny gardens in front of them. These were thought of as very posh! So there was a whole community within the yard and this created quite a sheltered existence, especially for the children. This was compounded by the fact that you could get everything you needed without going further than the end of Bondgate. There was a dairy, an ironmonger,

greengrocers, a grocer, a hairdresser, cake shops, a fish and chip shop, Chinese laundries, two churches, two cinemas and two pubs. If these were not enough, the famous Co-op Stores were just around the corner in Portland Place! So although the 'trollies' ran up and down Bondgate on overhead lines, the only times I can remember using them was to visit my Gran who lived at the other end of town.

I attended Holy Trinity School in Greenbank Road. This is now a block of flats. At the age of eleven I went to the Girls' High School in Cleveland Avenue. This really did seem as if I was 'going places'. Aged thirteen I decided to transfer to the Technical School in Gladstone Street to study Commercial Subjects. I still was not venturing far away from Bondgate!

It was no surprise then that, when I left school aged fifteen, I got a job as a junior shorthand typist at Leslie and Company in Woodlands Road. This was about 400 yards from Slater's Buildings. By the time I was eighteen years old, as the houses in the yard became empty they were not being re-let, so it was finally time to move. We moved just around the corner into Wycombe Street! Up until 1959, when I got married, I had lived, worked and played in an area of no more than half a square mile.

But to go back to the beginning. When I was seven years old my sister – having only been married for one year – died, aged twenty-one, after giving birth to a baby girl eleven days earlier. Eight weeks after my father died of a heart attack. That left my mother, a brother and myself. My brother, who was seventeen at the time, joined the Merchant Navy to ease matters. My mother, of course, had to go to work. (The widow's pension was 10s per week but you lost it if you earned more than £2.) For about twenty

years she worked in the fish and chip shop run by Billy Bishop and his sister, next to The Slater's Arms pub.

Times were hard for my family and most of the people I grew up with. A sense of humour was essential in order to survive. Despite the hardships, tragedies and tears of this small community, there was always a lot of laughter. Friendships were formed that lasted a lifetime. I have wonderful memories of street parties and Saturday morning cinema with the organ playing as it mysteriously rose from below. I also remember the neighbours who sold sweets from their front room and the bad-tempered dog who spent most of his time trying to jump over the wall between the two yards. The radio played all day with programmes like *ITMA*, *Workers Playtime*, *Dick Barton* and my favourite to this day, *The Archers*. Looking back, perhaps we were lucky to have lived in a yard.

Bondgate, 1930s. (Copyright, The Northern Echo)

It was only recently that I discovered that the house I had lived in, together with the one next door, was actually the first RC church built in 1786 at a time when Catholics were being discriminated against. It was built by Sir John Lawson of Catterick. He had helped the Carmelite Nuns flee from Belgium during the Napoleonic Wars. At that time the yard was known as Mass Yard. On completion of St Augustine's RC church in around 1827 there was no need for the chapel and it was turned into two cottages. Mass Yard was then renamed Weavers Yard, apparently after the profession of the people who lived there. It is not known how or why it became Slater's Buildings, but in 1963, the year my own daughter was born, it officially became known as the last inhabited town centre yard.

Mrs E. Wilson (née *Firth*)

Memories Of My Home Town

Being born in Darlington fifty years ago, I can remember some of the landmarks, good and bad, that can no longer be seen. For the first ten years of my life I lived in Leyburn Road. Just beyond that street was Martin's field, a place where the kids would play football and cricket, or chase each other playing Cowboys and Indians. We would run around pretending to be The Magnificent Seven, from the great film of that era. On reflection I was probably the one that no one can ever remember the name of. When it was too wet to play in the field, we would play hopscotch, rounders, lollipop sticks, or football-cricket in the front street. Even our parents would join in the fun because everyone was so neighbourly.

Further over Martin's field was the tip where rubbish from the Forge works would be dumped. We would sit for hours just waiting for the old train to trundle along to dump some rubbish, and rummage around believing that there might have been something worth finding.

Once past the tip, there were the railway lines where the old magnificent steam trains would speed past on their way to Edinburgh or London. Many a happy hour was spent just waiting and watching those trains go by, hoping to see the Flying Scotsman, or one of the Streaks. Beyond the railway lines were the marshy grounds, then nothing else until you got to Haughton, but now there are rows and rows of houses.

Just to the rear of Leyburn Road was the main road that led in and out of Darlington, when going, or coming from the north. That road has changed over the years, but not much. There are a few things that stick in the memory, things that can no longer be seen.

Firstly, there was the old trolley bus service that ran from the town centre, and then turned up the road at Cumberland Street, to take people up to the North Park. At the top of the street, the bus would turn around its little terminus, then return to the town. As a child, I can recall riding on that trolley bus many times.

Turning from Leyburn Road, and up Wensleydale Road, would take you to the main North Road and you could follow the trolley bus route to town. A hundred yards down the road, there was the church of Saint Paul's. It was in that very church that I was baptized, and attended on a Sunday morning for the service. Unfortunately, the church had to be demolished because it was gradually sinking into the ground that it

Brunswick Street car park, 1965. The power station cooling towers are in the background. (Copyright, The Northern Echo)

stood on, but it was a magnificent church when in all its glory, and the congregation on a Sunday was quite impressive.

As you walked down towards the town centre, you had to pass the North Road shops. To the children it was a mystical place where great trains were made, and we would try to stand on the wall and attempt to see one in the process of being built, although it was very rare that you could even see through the windows. To the hundreds of workers that headed there each day, carrying their bait boxes and flasks, it was their livelihood. It was the place where they would earn some money to feed their families. When the works closed down, it was devastating for a lot of families, and now that site is used for small independent firms.

Further down, just before going under Albert Road Bridge, there was a magnificent old house, with it's own grounds. It looked very impressive, and somewhat eerie at night, but it became a derelict building and

was demolished as well.

From almost anywhere in Darlington, the massive towers of the power station in Haughton Road could be seen. I can recall my father working there as a stoker and remember how black he looked when arriving home after cleaning out the boilers. Those huge cooling towers may not have been very beneficial for the environment, but they were a very impressive piece of architecture. It was sad for a lot of residents when those towers were finally reduced to rubble, because they had been a part of the heritage of Darlington for so long.

As a child, I can remember the old bus station in Leadyard. We would stand there waiting for the bus to whisk us off to Redcar or Saltburn for the day. Eventually, a wonderful, new, totally enclosed bus station was opened, right next to Feetham's field. This too, however, is now boarded up and awaiting someone's decision as to what will be done with it.

NORTHGATE POLICE STATION - 1910

Northgate Police Station, 1910. This is the original police station at Chestnut Street before it was relocated to its current site at Park Place. (Copyright, The Centre for Local Studies, Darlington Library)

Talking of Feetham's field brings back great memories of when the shows arrived. None of those rides were too great or too frightening, just the old carousels, bumper cars, waltzers, and sideshows, but what fun they provided. Gone is that field, where we built our bonfires and set off our fireworks, only to be replaced by a huge roundabout as part of the ring road.

From the age of ten to sixteen I lived across the road from Feetham's field. We had a little house in Beaumont Street. It was tiny, but it was our home. My mother bought that little house after she had sold our house in Leyburn Road for the princely sum of £1,500. Unfortunately, we only lived there for about five years, and then our house became a casualty of the council's Compulsory Purchase Act. All of those houses, along with others, like Park Place, were torn down to make way for progress. Granted, the area around Park Place made way for a new police station, which was moved from its site at the top of Chestnut Street, and a new fire station, and post office sorting office. But what of Beaumont Street and our tiny little house? Some thirty-odd years later, it's a grubby little pay and display car park, and no one has even bothered to resurface it. A sad end for that street of houses which their owners loved, but progress is progress, and nothing should stand in its way.

During that period of time there was plenty to do in Darlington. There were several cinemas to visit and see all of the top films, or the Saturday matinees for kids. At one time, there was the ABC, The Odeon, The Essoldo, The Regent, The Gaumont, and The Scala. Sadly, bingo fever took over and, one by one, they all closed down. I can remember going to the Fleapit (Scala), with my father, to see all the old silent movies that starred Buster Keaton, Charlie Chaplin, The Keystone Cops, and many others, then sitting through a session of bingo before seeing more silent movies.

When Sunday arrived you could walk to The South Park, North Lodge Park or North Park for a picnic. Each park had a magnificent bandstand where local brass bands would play their hearts out. Sadly, those beautiful centrepieces were left to wreck and ruin, and the parks are now rarely filled with many visitors. Mind you, the advent of television probably did not help the cause. I often wonder how children today would survive without modern technology. We did, and probably had some of the best times of our lives back then. We could always find something to do, or somewhere to go, and the beauty of it was that most of those activities would cost very little in terms of money.

Although I no longer live in my hometown, I still have a great affection for it.

Stephen Robinson

CHAPTER 2
Local Residents

High Row, Darlington *by John Binney Gibbs (1859-1935). This is a view of High and Low Rows in 1896. William Sewell was fifty-two years old at this time and at the height of his several successful careers. He and his family would be very familiar with such a peaceful scene. (Copyright Gordon Coates from Borough of Darlington Art gallery Collection)*

William Sewell, 1844-1935

On 30 January 1935 the front-page news in the *Northern Despatch*, one of Darlington's four main newspapers at the time, was the newly fallen blanket of snow covering the town. Children were having an energetic snowball fight in Bondgate School playground and motorists had been obliged to fit ski-chains to their vehicles. There was also much moaning about the inconvenience of wet feet and the need for gumboots.

Inside the paper amidst the local and countrywide news there was a whole column reporting the death of Mr William Sewell of Darlington. He had died the previous evening, the day of his ninety-first birthday at his home in Stanhope Road. The article calls him a 'retired newspaper managing director', but this was only one of the many ways in which William Sewell had contributed to the life of Darlington. From the early days of the railway, throughout it's fast developing Victorian era, and on to the 1930s William Sewell had certainly been, as the paper says, 'one of Darlington's best known men.'

William was born in the Leadyard, down by the River Skerne, just past St Cuthbert's church, in 1844. His parents are named on his baptismal certificate as John and Mary-Anne and his father's trade is listed as a currier. Their families had originally been farmers from Blackwell, Coniscliffe and Houghton le Side, but in common with many inhabitants of the countryside had moved in to town during the early nineteenth century. The town was still quite small, bounded by the Skerne and extending up to Skinnergate, Blackwellgate and Bondgate. Between these areas were lots of yards often crammed with large families and groups of workers who had come in from around the country as well as Scotland and Ireland looking for seasonal work and work on the railways. The first Public Health Act was not to be passed until 1848 and there was still no clean water supply to the town and no sewer system. Even though as a currier, William's father probably had some business standing, people living in the Leadyard would have had to use wells, which were often polluted, or river water, and would have to share earthen toilets. Each yard usually had it's own shops and one of these would have been a butcher. Skins were tanned down at the Skerne by hand and so there would have been offal disposed of next to living quarters as well. William must have been a fighter from his earliest days to survive the high infant mortality rate of the time!

The Sewells were able to send their son to St Cuthbert's School, which was in the Leadyard, and he finished his education at the age of twelve. He was impressive enough to land a job straight away as an office boy to the clerk of the Darlington Board of Guardians, Mr William Morrison, and so started on a career which was to take him far away from his father's trade of currier.

From this early start William progressed to working in the Darlington Office of the *Richmond and Ripon Chronicle* and when only just in his twenties became well known for his energy and enthusiasm, visiting surrounding villages and hamlets regularly in search of news. His bright red hair and zest for whatever he was doing earned him the nickname of 'the red hot fire-brand'. In 1886, when he was still only twenty-two, he became a commercial manager of the joint *Darlington and Stockton Times* and the *Richmond and Ripon Chronicle*. He worked for Henry King Spark originally but the paper got into financial difficulties when Spark became bankrupt. It was eventually bailed out by a group of four investors and William was invited to take over as the new manager. One of his first actions was to reduce the price of the paper to 1d, which was done as an effort to make the news available to everyone, but would have also had a great effect on sales figures! *The Northern Echo*, which was a daily paper, was famous for keeping its price down to a halfpenny and the evidence of its large circulation could have influenced William's ideas for extending the availability of the weekly *Darlington and Stockton Times*. It certainly worked, as sales of the paper are reported to have 'increased twentyfold' whilst he was in charge. During 1890 there was an editorial split on the issue of Irish Home Rule and the shareholders asked William for advice on what to do. He advised that Arthur Pease and John Bowman should buy out the rest of them and they did this, leaving William charged with the weekly management of the paper. He ran it with a series of editors, except at one point when he actually edited, as well as managed it for a few years. He remained there for another thirty-eight years after the Home Rule debate had been sorted out, finally retiring in 1928.

In 1874 William agreed to take the position of Registrar for the Board of Guardians and held this position for a long time, working as Darlington Registrar of Births, Deaths and Marriages for another forty years. This job also made him Vaccination Officer and he is mentioned in the Guardians Report of 1901 as detailing that there were 677 live births in the previous year and of these 81 had died before reaching vaccination. Another 23 had obtained certificates of 'conscientious objection' to vaccination, showing that some people obviously had worries about vaccinating their children, even 100 years ago.

Another event that William was also involved in through most of its heyday was the Darlington Horse and Dog Show which was described as 'the largest, best one day show in England.' It was a very prestigious event in late Victorian times and people travelled from far and wide in their carriages and tandems to attend. Although not a Quaker himself, William was closely associated with Arthur Pease who was one of the Darlington and Stockton shareholders and with other members of the Pease family through his position as Secretary of the Horse and Dog Show. It was held in various Pease family residences. These included Pierremont, Woodside and Hummersknott, which is now Carmel Technology College. William was secretary for thirty years and ran it with the financial and practical support of the Pease family. During this time he was also a Freemason and became Master of the Restoration Lodge, which is one of the oldest in the area and would have helped him consolidate contacts with many local businessmen.

His interest in all things new in that fast-moving era of inventions meant that the motorcar was bound to catch his attention. He became a member of the board of W.E. Dove & Co. Motor and Electrical Engineers who had opened a garage in the Salt Yard, just off Bondgate. William was involved with them until just before his death in 1935. He often took motor rides to the surrounding countryside and revisited places he had travelled to by horse and carriage in the days when he was building up the *Darlington and Stockton Times*.

In 1869, when he was twenty-five years old, William married Mary, a young lady from the village of East Cowton. By the mid-1870s they had two sons, Francis and Charles, and they were financially stable enough to be able to buy a plot of land from the Duke of Cleveland and build their dream house. The Duke's land stretched from Skinnergate out to the west of the existing town and it became the first big middle-class housing development in

Darlington. Many of the names of streets were taken from the Duke's family – with Vane Terrace, Cleveland Avenue and Terrace, Stanhope Road and of course Duke Street all well known today. The area must have been a thriving building site in the 1870s as the College for Training Young Ladies as Elementary Teachers, now used as Darlington Arts Centre, opened at that time and all the surrounding streets were under construction. Stanhope Green was placed in front of the college and was only accesible to the resident key holders – as it was bordered by impressive railings and ornate iron gates.

William and Mary moved in to their large double-fronted house in Stanhope Road in the late 1870s and by 1891 it housed a family of three children, including their young daughter Mary, and three servants, two of whom 'lived in'. A manservant, James Marcell, lived with the family and a young woman named Sarah A. Rose is listed as being 'a woman living on her own means' in the 1891 census. It's possible that she was a nanny or governess for the children or even a lodger – as many of the bigger houses had these. The Sewells also had a long-serving family retainer called Jane Barnett who stayed with the family until William died in 1935. At some point around this time there is also mention of a third son in the family who was also called William. Mary and William senior celebrated their Golden Wedding in 1919 and he was honoured with a presentation from the *Darlington and Stockton Times*. In the report from the time it is remarked that, although William had been so successful in his public and working life, with the rise of the paper, the success of the Horse and Dog Show, his work as Registrar and also with Dove's Motors to his credit, his private life had not

had such luck.

By 1919 all but one of his children had died. Frank, the eldest had left Darlington to live and work in Wallasey in Cheshire and was a grandfather himself. William's second child, Charles, had died in Chicago and William junior had become a promising artist and illustrator, but enlisted in the Bedfordshire Regiment at the beginning of the Great War and was killed in Flanders in 1917. His only daughter Mary was married for a short while and died young, leaving a granddaughter for William and Mary to raise. Tragically she caught influenza during the great epidemic of 1918 and died. There were, however, four grandchildren and two great-grandchildren left to brighten their later years.

Mary died in 1924, and after his retirement in 1928 William took regular walks about the town. He became known as a famous local face and a mine of information about nineteenth-century Darlington. He still travelled about extensively to surrounding towns and villages as well and was known never to go to bed before 12.45 a.m. rising at 7.30 a.m. promptly to review his post and papers before breakfast.

On that snowy day in January 1935 there was only William, Jane Barnett, then eighty-one, and a nurse in the house in Stanhope Road. His energy and forward thinking can be summed up by a quote that he gave when asked by a reporter to describe the 'old days'. He replied that 'Those times are the bad old times – it is the present times that are the good times.'

In his obituary the *Darlington and Stockton Times* said that, 'he maintained a sense of humour that never deserted him. He never allowed the sordid and tragic to obtrude in his newspaper. His view was that there was enough sorrow in the world without seeking to emphasize it'

William Sewell's life spanned the Victorian and Edwardian eras in Darlington and these were a time of great change. He always moved with it, and certainly earned the paper's description as 'one of the best known men in his own town.'

Alice T. Potter
Prize Winner

The Sad Case Of Lady Jarrett

In Feethams in Darlington, where today the council offices and the bus station are, there used to stand the ancient Manor House of the Bishops of Durham. It had been one of the few buildings of the old town, along with St Cuthbert's church, which had survived the great fire of 1585. It had a long history, parts of it dating back to the twelfth century; its last use was as a workhouse, before being pulled down in1870.

An old building such as this was bound to collect a legend or two over the years, and the Bishop's Manor House had a particularly gruesome and bloody one to tell. It concerned a certain unfortunate Lady Jarrett who resided here in the seventeenth century.

In the 1640s the country was in turmoil as the two sides in the Civil War fought each other. The Cavaliers, supporting King Charles I, and Cromwell's Roundheads clashed in battles all over the English countryside.

In Darlington, as in many other towns, soldiers would have been a common sight. And according to our legend, some of these decided that the substantial Bishop's Manor House looked like a good place to do a bit of looting.

On breaking into the house, they came face to face with the formidable Lady Jarrett who lived there at the time and who obstinately refused to hand over any money or valuables to the intruders. But the greedy thieves noticed that she was wearing an expensive-looking ring on one of her fingers. Grabbing the unfortunate lady, they yanked at her hand to try to pull off the ring. But it was to no avail.

And here the legend becomes particularly lurid. Frustrated and angry, the soldiers took their weapons and hacked away savagely, severing her arm completely from her body. Then, triumphant, they carried off the gory limb, ring and all. Poor Lady Jarrett, in her dying throes, covered in blood, staggered to the wall, and sank lifeless to the floor, leaving ghastly crimson prints of bloody thumb and fingers on the wall as she fell. Strange to tell, no amount of scrubbing could get rid of those horrible stains; whitewashing was tried to cover them over, with equally litle success.

More than 300 years later in 1870 Mr Richard Luck was demolishing the Manor House to make way for Luck's Square which he was building on the site. In a letter, he wrote that he came across the room where Lady Jarrett had been murdered and found that the macabre bloodstains, which could not be washed off, were still visible.

While he was working away, he heard footsteps coming out of this room, and, although he could not see anybody, he felt instinctively that it must be Lady Jarrett herself.

'I could hear,' he wrote, 'the rustle of her silk dress, and she came close until I could feel her breath and her dress as she stooped over my shoulder to see what I was doing.'

The Manor House was used as a workhouse in the final era of its history before it was pulled down. And to the inmates at the time, the ghost of Lady Jarrett was a familiar and much loved spirit. She was even known to make coffee for them; and when any of them were suddenly taken ill, Lady Jarrett came to the rescue, when the rustle of her silken dress was heard as she floated along the corridors to bang on the matron's door to come to help. The inmates knew that she lived in the passage which ran between the Manor House and St Cuthbert's church. And though everybody knew she was a friendly sort of ghost, nobody ever dared explore this particular passage.

In his demolition work, Mr Luck must have blocked it up. Never again has the ghastly rustle of silk been heard; the story of Lady Jarrett and her terrible encounter and death have passed into the realms of legend.

Jim Foster

Mary Clement, The Postmaster's Daughter

One of the most delightful stories that I have read regarding Darlington in days gone by can be found in *Longstaffe's History and Antiquities of Darlington*. Around 1730 Mr Edward Walpole, who had become known by the ladies in Italy as 'The Handsome Englishman', returned from his travels on the continent. He was the son of England's first Prime Minister, Sir Robert Walpole.

On his return to England he lived in Pall Mall, London. Almost opposite, was a ready-made linen warehouse where gentlemen procured items for their wardrobe. A very respectable lady, named Mrs Rennie, ran the shop with her assistants. One of these assistants was a very pretty girl called Mary Clement. Her father was the postmaster of Darlington and he had a very large family. Consequently, his daughter, Mary, was apprenticed to Mrs Rennie. Mary Clement's family had little to give her in way of clothes or money.

Mr Walpole would visit the shop and spend time chatting to the ladies. But the one who could make him forget all the beauties of the English Court was the attractive Mary Clement. Mr Walpole often gave her little presents, being careful not to alarm the girl or her mistress who exacted the strictest morality from the young persons in her care.

Mrs Rennie, however, was a shrewd observer and she began to suspect that more than polite conversation was beginning to form. She believed that this would not be to the honour of her apprentice. She advised Mary's father of her suspicions, and he came from Darlington to collect his daughter and carry her away from temptation. The good old man tearfully advised Mary that he was aware of possible problems with Mr Walpole. He said that he would take her home where by good clean living, she may, in time, marry some good tradesman from her own town.

Mary listened to her father, and in appearance agreed with him and left the room in order to prepare for her trip back to Darlington. But Mary had other plans that day, and while her father and her mistress were in deep conversation behind the shop, she slipped quietly out, and without hat or coat ran directly to Pall Mall, and Sir Edward's house. The porter, who knew her, admitted her, even though his master was absent. She impatiently awaited Edward's return, and when the moment arrived, he entered and exclaimed with great joy, 'You...here?' Her explanations were given in privacy, and later our fair fugitive sat at the head of his table, and never after left it.

Now the fruits of this joyous union were, firstly, Laura, who became Mrs Keppel. Their second child was Maria, who became Lady Walgrave and later the Duchess of Gloucester. The third child became Lady Dysart and the fourth, Colonel Walpole. Mary died during, or soon after, the birth of her fourth child. Sir Edward's grief at the loss of his beloved Mary was so great that he refused all future offers of marriage and dedicated himself to his children and their education. He had often wished to marry his beloved Mary, but his father Sir Robert Walpole, the Prime Minister, refused this using many forms of political blackmail. It was said that if Mary had survived Sir Robert, she would indeed have been Lady Walpole.

In 1758 Mary's eldest daughter, Laura, became the wife of the Hon. Frederick Keppel, brother to the Earl of Albermale, and later Bishop of Exeter. The young and attractive daughters of Mary Clement took on a new role after Laura's marriage, and they were now accepted into a society in which their mother had never been allowed to move. The sisters of the Earl of Albermale were their constant companions and introduced them to people of quality and fashion.

No one had watched their upward progress more than the Earl of Waldegrave. This very noble man had long cherished a great passion for Maria. He was also a very proud man who struggled with his passion and his pride. As is always the case, however, love conquers all, and although not a young man by any means, he professed his feelings to the lovely Maria. The result

was marriage in 1759 and she took on the role of a good wife in every way. After about five years, his Lordship was attacked by smallpox and this proved fatal. Sweet Maria, daughter of Mary Clement of Darlington, became a young widow of rank and beauty. Had Lord Waldegrave possessed the advantage of youth, his passing could not have been more heartfelt by his good wife.

Eventually she emerged from mourning, and love and admiration followed her everywhere. She refused many offers of marriage, but the daughter of Mary Clement was destined for royalty! The Duke of Gloucester was not to be resisted and two children, a prince and princess, resulted from their marriage. So it came within the bounds of probability that the daughter of the postmaster of Darlington, might one day have swayed the British sceptre – now that is quite a thought!

Ron Watson

The Journey: The Story Of A Darlington Family

The journey was short, just three miles, but in the change of lifestyle the distance was immeasurable.

My great-great-grandfather, Edward Wood, was born in 1813 in the village of Hurworth-on-Tees. He was a linen weaver just as his father Christopher and grandfather Simon had been before him. In August 1840 he married Elizabeth Jameson from the neighbouring village of Neasham. They were married at All Saints church, Hurworth, when their son, William, was nearly two years old. In the mid-nineteenth century it was not uncommon for women to be pregnant or to have children when they

Mary Wood, born 1852.

Ellen Wood, born 1856.

married, as a man needed to know that his wife could bear him sons. However, the most probable reason they were not married earlier was simply economic. The 1840s, known as the hungry forties, was a time of great unemployment and starvation as the mechanisation and industrialisation of Britain made many of the old cottage industries redundant. As a handloom weaver Edward was almost certainly out of work.

Some historians believe the linen weavers in Hurworth were descended from French Huguenots who immigrated to England to escape religious persecution in France. It is possible that the ancestors of Edward Wood were indeed Huguenots. The churchyard at All Saints church in Hurworth bears tombstones to the Wood family and the same names occur in each generation.

Edward's luck changed with the development of the railways. He was given a job as points man with the Newcastle and Berwick Railway Company and, most wonderful of all, a house went with the job. I can imagine him running almost all of the three miles back to Neasham to tell Elizabeth of their good fortune.

The house still stands, one of a block of seven, in an elevated position on Haughton Road near the bottom of Hundens Lane. When Edward and Elizabeth moved into their little 'Railway Cottage' it was probably newly built and Edward would work the points at the crossing. The road we now know as Haughton Road was simply called Haughton Lane, and was on the outskirts of the town leading to Haughton village. There was no St James church, no Albert Hill, but the farms at Nestfield and Hundens would be familiar to Elizabeth and Edward.

Their family grew. After William came Annie in 1840, Elizabeth in 1842, Edward (Ned) in 1845, Jane in 1850, Mary (Polly) in 1852, Ellen in 1856 who became my great-grandmother, and Sarah in 1860. All, except William, were born in that little cottage on Haughton Lane. Edward worked his way up through the ranks of the railway and became an Express engine driver. By this time William had started work and was also employed by the railway as an engine cleaner.

From William's birth, in 1838, to 1860 they had eight children who survived their early years. The children were baptized in St Cuthbert's church and probably attended schools on Bank Top, the Bank Top Railway School or Bridge Street British School. Although education was not compulsory until the late 1870s, the children could all read and write. Their father, Edward, writes in a fair hand on his wedding certificate, while Elizabeth, his wife, could only manage a cross. As the girls grew older they were sent into service, Mary was employed by Henry Pease and stayed for a time at his castle in Stanhope, eventually becoming housekeeper at Brinkburn. Ellen and Sarah were apprenticed as seamstresses while Ned, once again, worked on the railway. After Edward's death Elizabeth worked as an attendant in the First Class Ladies Waiting Room at Bank Top Station, a job that had much status in her family's eyes.

The family stayed in Darlington and it is interesting to note that for five generations they lived in the Haughton and Eastbourne area of Darlington, only moving to the outskirts of the town in the last five years. The Woods are an ordinary, working class family, having worked at The Darlington Forge, Lily Laundry, Rise Carr Rolling Mills

and Patons & Baldwins. My grandmother was a housemaid at Elm Ridge for the Hodgkin family and at one time two sisters Kate and Emma lived at The Lodge on Haughton Road and were lodge keepers for Eastmount. At the turn of the nineteenth century one great aunt was housekeeper at Brinkburn for the Pease family. Since then there have been electricians, railway workers, secretaries, a police sergeant, a detective, a plumber, a university lecturer, civil servants, soldiers, and one chief cashier at the town hall.

For 150 years the descendents of that young couple from Hurworth have lived, worked and died in Darlington. Now in the year 2001 the great-great-great-great-grandsons of Edward and Elizabeth Wood attend school in Darlington. Who knows what their future will be? Whatever Darlington's future, I hope that there will be a member of the Wood family somewhere in the town.

Maureen Snowball

The Bradfords Of Darlington

If while walking along Millbank Road, Darlington you should see an elderly chap smartly saluting a house, please do not ring 999 requesting men in white coats with restraining equipment.

The splendid residence 'Benwell' was where the Bradford family lived and from it, in August 1914, went their four sons to do their duty for King and country. Only one was to return.

The head of the family was George Bradford, a hard northern, mining engineer who played a major role in the growing industrialisation of County Durham and

Darlington Queen Elizabeth Grammar School football team. Roland Bradford is the captain in the centre with the ball. Eight of these thirteen boys are known to have died between 1914-1918.

Darlington. Late in life he married a gentle woman from Kent named Amy Andrews. They had four sons and after a gap a daughter, Amy.

By today's standards the father brought the boys up harshly but fairly and they developed into perfect physical specimens. All excelled at more than one sport. Thomas, the eldest and the only one to survive the war, once scored 207 not out. George, the only one not to join the Durham Light Infantry, was considered the best boxer the Royal Navy ever produced. James and Roland were excellent footballers and horse riders.

Two other factors made them what they were. At every opportunity their father read tales to them of men doing their duty and

battling against great odds, such as *Horatio at the Bridge* and *Pilgrims Progress*. Their maternal grandfather, despite his age and distance to travel, came as often as possible to see his grandchildren. He regaled them with accounts of how he had sparred with the great pugilists of the day, Tom Sayers and Jem Mace. He would don the gloves and show them all the arts of self-defence.

They were a religious family and not only did the boys attend Holy Trinity in Woodlands Road but they were active in running the Boys Brigade. A plaque in the church is a touching memorial.

Thomas somehow survived years of bitter trench fighting with the Durham Light Infantry as a Captain and was honoured with the award of DSO, a high decoration.

He was to show a different type of courage in 1922 when he stood as a Conservative candidate in Seaham Harbour against the famous socialist, Sydney Webb. He polled over 8,000 votes, probably from ex-DLIs.

Mother Amy, widowed in 1912, was to receive her first dreaded telegram from the War Office in May 1917. James had been constantly fighting in the trenches, except for invalid leave after being wounded on the infamous Somme. He soon returned to battle and won a Military Cross for bravery but was to die from further wounds.

George was the last of the three brothers to die. He was born on St George's Day 1887 and he died on St George's Day 1918. He had already demonstrated his courage pre-war in 1912 when he risked his life to save an unknown cabin boy in the Channel.

A raid was planned jointly by the Army and Navy on the Zeebrugge port. There were no commandos in the First World War but hand-picked men were to be used in key roles. George was a volunteer. When the modified Liverpool ferryboat, *Iris,* was having difficulty being secured to the mole the British losses on her were severe. Although not part of his allotted duties, Lt-Com. Bradford seized an anchor, climbed a derrick and leapt on to the mole. Admiral Sir Roger Keyes wrote to his mother 'your son's act of glorious self-sacrifice stood out alone.'

George was awarded a posthumous VC. His mother went to Buckingham Palace to receive it from King George V, wearing the VC previously awarded to her youngest son, the legendary Roland.

Roland Boys Bradford was exceptional from boyhood at the Queen Elizabeth Grammar School. He went to France in September 1914 as a twenty-two-year-old Second Lieutenant in the 2nd Battalion of Durham Light Infantry. When he was killed in action in November 1917 he was a Brigadier General in command of the 18th Infantry Brigade and the holder of the MC and VC.

No one in the British Army ever had such rapid promotion on pure merit and remember he did not come from a military background and had no friends in high places. No one has ever become a General aged twenty-five or is likely to. His courage, coolness and inspirational leadership were noted and remarked upon from the highest to the lowest-ranking private. At a time when squaddies normally received scant attention, Roland always thought first of his men's well-being. Out of the line their rest and recreation were his prime concern.

In letters home to influential people he asked for comforts for his men such as candles, socks, cake and kippers. He requested medals for a football competition he was organizing. He formed a band, begged sheet music and organized a concert party, The Green Diamonds, and performed in it.

He was wounded several times as he led from the front but refused to leave his posts. Already mentioned in Dispatches and awarded the MC he was to receive the VC for an episode on the Somme in September 1916.

He was promoted to Lieutenant Colonel and placed in command of the 9th Battalion who were heavily involved in a fierce attack. During this attack the senior officers of the neighbouring 6th Battalion were all killed or wounded. Roland took command of both battalions and fearlessly rallied them both and succeeded in securing the flank.

The plaque in Holy Trinity bears the names of the three brothers who paid the

A plaque commemorating the life of Roland Boys Bradford located in St Cuthbert's church.

supreme sacrifice. It also carries the words 'Abide with Me' which have special relevance to Roland. Every evening, whether in a shell hole with a few men or in trenches with hundreds, he would lead the men in singing this hymn. It became such a tradition that it was later officially adopted by the Durham Light Infantry.

In the 150 years since Queen Victoria authorised the VC award for valour less than 1,400 have been presented worldwide. Two of these came to one house in Millbank Road in Darlington. Perhaps after reading this I might not be the only one to salute 'Benwell' in passing.

Allan Newman

Eddie King, Men's Outfitter

A cold Advent, five years before the commencement of the Great War, was the scene of my father's birth. A plain and simple inner terrace house in Backhouse Street provided the shelter for new baby Eddie. Charlie, his father and my paternal grandfather, worked as a 'nightsoilman' – using the midnight hours to clear away the waste from the earth closets of neighbouring houses. Edith or 'Edie', his mother and my paternal grandmother, was a fearsome lady! Perhaps nine children, taking in washing and caring for the neighbours' children were enough to create a permanent frown. Grandma generally wore black clothes topped by a black straw hat whose brim was surrounded by artificial fruit. Backhouse Street was reasonably near to the foul smelling River Skerne. It was surrounded by hundreds of other terraced houses. The soot and smoke of those many coal fires doing its best to blot out the landscape. For those going to and from their daily work it was a constant battle to find their front doors, especially if the day was wet and dingy. In December 1909 'work' was to be found at the nearby Denham's Foundry, the Railway Plant or in Albert Road at the 'Forge'. For female workers jobs as shop assistants or the gruelling task of being 'in service' appeared to be the norm, or else trying to cope with the dry, dusty atmosphere of Pease's Mill.

My father was born into these situations, a sickly baby. My grandma was poor. Making ends meet did not include eating the 'right things' to see out pregnancy. Consequently my father, as he began to walk, developed rickets. His shinbones became bent and miss shapen. He spent his early years either on the living room floor or else being pushed around by his brothers in a carriage. Schooling came at eight or nine years of age in Beaumont Street. I marvel at what he eventually achieved after four years in school. Father left at thirteen to tackle his first job.

In 1922 the scene was one of grimy cobblestones, horse and cart traffic, wooden framed market stalls and hissing gas lamps. The Market Place, or more precisely, East Row, was always of a hustle and bustle! My father was employed by Titus Atkinson to sell menswear – shirts, braces, socks, loose collars, suits etc. between the hours of 4.00 p.m. and 9.00 p.m. during evenings and on Saturdays. T. Atkinson Hatter & Outfitter was situated under the Covered Market, at Nos 6 and 7 East Row, sandwiched between public toilets and a

fruit wholesalers. Seventy-four years later the four main windows may still be seen, displaying a variety of camping gear and outdoor clothing. Father supervised four trestle tables – one in front of each window – neatly laid out with men's clothing. A hand bell was rung promptly at 9.00 p.m. at the close of trading, but not before some clothing had disappeared without being paid for! Purloined suits and shirts did not, however, spoil my father's chances of being permanently employed by Titus.

At the age of fifteen, in 1924, Eddie was offered the chance to serve the public under the close scrutiny of Titus and, shortly afterwards, Mr Foster. In his young days Eddie was quite a 'dandy'. Whilst 'in the shop' he was always smartly dressed with a permanent top-pocket handkerchief in place. His growing confidence meant that a short walk to Barclay's Bank on High Row was punctuated by many conversations, as his circle of friends grew. Of course, he was very much the new boy and out to impress! His early ability to sell clothing and keep a tidy shop attracted the manager of Burras and Peake, Men's Outfitters. Eddie was lured away from East Row for just eighteen months to a shop carrying out similar trade towards the bottom left corner of Bondgate, nearly opposite the former entrance to Queen Street. However, it has to be said that Atkinsons did not prosper in my father's absence. Falling trade and poor bookkeeping meant that, one day in 1925/26 Mr Foster hurried across to Bondgate to bargain for Eddie's release and return to the shop 'under the market'.

So began the happiest and most fulfilling time in my father's life. He had recovered from seriously poor physical health, learnt the ins and outs of retail selling and taught himself how to organize income and expenditure ledgers and was making good friends with other market traders.

As the new manager of T. Atkinson Hatter & Outfitter what did he inherit? Much of my childhood was spent exploring this 'Dickensian' shop and its quaint fittings. The floor space was divided into three separate shops. The front shop was the place for transactions great and small. Farmers demanding 'luck money' whilst at the same time pulling out a wad of white five pound notes from back pockets. Caps and neckties were displayed for the browsing public whilst Eddie secured parcels with brown paper and string. In his waistcoat pocket he kept a small pair of scissors, always sharp enough to deal with the most fibrous string! The side shop was reserved for heavy working trousers, boiler suits, dustcoats, jackets and heavy-duty suits – often of Harris tweed. The back shop held the most fascination for me. Smooth and level surfaces topped tiers of drawers, ideal for racing toy cars along! Circular tables wer constructed around roof-supporting pillars and the pillars were disguised as three-sided mirrors. Everything wooden was deep and richly coloured rosewood. In the corner was the office – very Victorian in structure as befitted a shop constructed in 1863. All floors were bare wood and the electric lighting left much to be desired.

Monday and Saturday were the busiest of days. The Monday Cattle Market saw Eddie coping with large numbers of farmers some of whom wanted to try on trousers. Without suitable changing rooms if, as a small boy, I was pushing cars around the rosewood counters I would be ushered out into the front shop, curtains pulled across the doorway and the customer left to their privacy!

As shop manager my father, Eddie, had many brushes with local personalities. Once, in his early days as shop assistant, he was confronted with a lady customer carrying a square-shaped box. 'In here are two live hens, look after them until I've done my shopping!' With that she bustled out of the shop and across the Market Square. Eddie relates that he continued the usual tasks of dusting shelves, entering up the ledger and serving customers. However the 'temporary errand boy' was not able to keep his fingers off the wooden peg that secured the hen's cage. The next thing, two fat hens struggled out of their box and flew out of the open shop door! Shouts and screams in Tubwell Row heralded their progress as shopping bags tumbled and vehicles swerved. Meanwhile my father wondered how on earth he would keep his reputation. Some people are very adept at catching hens! So it was that creatures were returned to captivity before the lady returned to claim them. The shop had two entrances separated by two display windows. A favourite game of drunks was to enter by one door and stagger out through the other whilst shoppers stood and gaped. If the drunk collapsed in front of a window, so blocking the public's gaze, Eddie would lock the doors and hurry up to the town clock pedestrian crossing. Once there he would request that the white-gloved and white-armed policeman on point duty come and remove the offending man to the cells in Northgate.

Eddie knew Geordie Fawbert, he also knew Geordie's wife. She sold fresh fish from a stall outside the shop. One afternoon another very drunk man reeled across to the fish stall and began saying some very naughty things about the fish on display. Geordie's wife attempted to take no notice, but to no avail. Eddie watched as this small

Eddie King outside his shop 'T. Atkinson Hatter & Outfitter' located under the covered market until 1977.

lady with forearms the size of hams strolled round to the front of her stall and landed a huge round-arm punch to the drunk's jaw! He was dragged by the scruff of the neck, well away from the fish and to the feet of a policeman who had been alerted to the fracas.

Despite his hard work, Eddie's shop never was properly modernized. He was issued with a key for a toilet situated under the Horse Market steps into the Covered Market, filled his kettle at a stand pipe along the tunnel that stretched from the archway under the market steps, along from the shop, and was warmed for very many years by a gas ring on the floor of the back shop. He generally saught comfort by cycling home for lunch. Having ninety minutes to cycle to

Sandriggs, in Faverdale, eat lunch and return to remove the cardboard announcement from the door – 'back after lunch'.

Selling clothes to men and boys did have its compensations. As the shop became well known for quality merchandise and good service, so people called in to seek Eddie's advice on a number of issues. The town's clergy, especially Baptist Ministers, would sit around a back shop table and discuss theology; friends would ask to leave heavy shopping while hurried meals were eaten and buses caught into the Dales. Very often, too, those who just wanted to discuss the 'Quakers' football team or the council's latest decisions could be seen contentedly leaning against the front shop counters.

STAITHES

Chapters from the history of a seafaring town

JOHN HOWARD

STAITHES

CHAPTERS FROM THE HISTORY OF A SEAFARING TOWN.

by JOHN HOWARD

This comprehensive and fascinating account outlines the growth of a unique and remarkable community.

The story of Staithes and its development are traced across the centuries from its origins in the inland Domesday settlement of Seaton to its eminence two hundred years ago, when it was the largest fishing station in the north of England and numbered its fishermen in hundreds. The economy geared to the catching, processing and transporting of fish supported an infrastructure of closely knit, inter-related families, chapels, schools, benevolent and friendly societies. So detailed are the descriptions of the many aspects of life in the town, that most Staithes families feature in the narrative. During the closing decades of the nineteenth century, when smuggling was rampant, Staithes experienced a period of prosperity and the nearby alum works at Boulby provided a further catalyst to the economy of the town, which was well known for producing seafarers of repute.

As the nineteenth century progressed, several external forces combined to undermine the prosperity of the town, which hitherto had, through its shop keepers and tradesmen, provided goods and services for the surrounding countryside.

Author John Howard, who is descended from Staithes stock, writes about his birth place with authority and sensitivity. Over the years, he has gathered together a rich hoard of anecdotes, recollections and reminiscences and these he combines effectively with results of his research, drawn from local and national archives and sources overseas.

This book, which contributes significantly to the local history of the area, will not only appeal to a wide readership, but will also become a valuable work of reference.

Published by John Howard
13 Tibby Butts, Scalby,
Scarborough.
N. Yorkshire YO13 0RF

Telephone 01723 363626

PRICE £9.95
P&P £2.00

Available from:

Holman's Bookshop, 19-21 Skinner Street, Whitby. YO21 3AH Tel: 01947 602372
Guisborough Bookshop, 4 Chalenor Street, Guisborough. TS14 6QD Tel: 01287 610179
Sotheran's, 14-16 Queen Street, Redcar. TS10 1AF Tel: 01642 490401
Also available from John Howard (Author)

There were callers who required just that little bit extra. A coffee stall situated on the corner of East Row and Tubwell Row could always be relied upon to offer a steady supply of creamy coffee and rich brown tea. As a boy I recall being sent out to bring back trays of drinks for those 'special visitors'. Commercial travellers from distant parts of Yorkshire and Lancashire came and went from Leeds, Huddersfield, Hebden Bridge and Manchester. Many of my neckties were free samples given by a traveller grateful for a substantial order! Billy Wake, whose main task was to wind-up the town clock, was a regular visitor. So too was 'Clarkie', Mr Clarke the Markets Superintendent. He and Eddie often talked about the state of the markets – both covered and open.

During the latter days of trading 'under the market', this constant stream of visitors provided some consolation to Eddie. He had spent a total of fifty-three years creating a good business only to experience the cruel realities of a town becoming populated by larger clothing stores that promoted lower prices. Daily takings dropped alarmingly and so, in 1977, my father put up the shop's wooden shutters for the last time. Press photographers and reporters from the *Northern Echo* produced features; customers expressed disbelief and many of the shop's fixtures and fittings were despatched to Beamish Open Air Museum.

Developers moved in to 'lay' the ghost of Titus Atkinson and Darlington witnessed the passing of its last Victorian menswear shop.

Peter King
Prize Winner

Butterfield The Barber

The following tales give an insight into working class life in Cockerton in the 1950s and are related through the eyes of a boy, namely the barber's son, Frank. The title of this story is a misnomer in itself, for the premises comprised a one room shop situated at No. 2 Prior Street, Cockerton and was universally known as 'Fred's'.

I saw Dad on Sundays only, never thinking to ask why. The rest of the week he disappeared from home at 7.45 a.m. Returning well after my bedtime. What a work ethic that man had. From starting his business in 1949 until he retired in 1978 he laboured twelve hours a day in that one room in order to bring up his family.

Fred was uncompromising in three areas, namely in his skill as a barber, as proprietor he was absolute master of his ship and in his politeness towards his customers. It should perhaps be explained that youngsters and mothers with small children were attended to before teatime; thereafter the shop became a male preserve.

Now, this is where my tale really begins, once a month I saw Fred at work, 'haircut day', and being 'family' I always had to wait until last. I learned to love *The Archers* which was on the radio at 6.45 p.m. and meant I should be 'on the chair' by 8.00 p.m. After helping to clean-up, I would be home by 9.00 p.m.

Now Fred's place really was a village institution. I cannot remember a visit without the place being crammed with workers. Flat caps, scarves, blue boiler-suited workers from the Rail, the Whessoe or the Forge. It was generally accepted that the functional purpose of a visit to Fred's, took a secondary position to the pleasure derived from merely being in the shop. Fred's, it should be explained, was a forum, a place where the working classes could without fear of favour or without censure from their peers, expound their views and opinions on politics, work, religion, football, in fact anything they chose to discuss. Every customer on entering the shop knew he would have the opportunity to listen to other peoples views and have the chance to expound his own. Once invited into the barber's chair and after a few opening words from Fred, 'Now what will it be sir?' the client knew the floor was his, a stage upon which personal opinions could be given to an appreciative audience.

From my corner of the shop, which I shared with a toy mouse that kept the children amused and the gas ring, on which Fred always kept a mug of lukewarm over-stewed tea, I was able to view the proceedings. Of the customers themselves, no faces were to be seen, only caps perched apparently without substance from behind copies of the *Daily Mirror*, *The Northern Echo* or *Northern Despatch*.

The true business of the shop, an exchange of conversation and information, was conducted on a two-way basis, the speaker on the 'Chair' and the 'Response'. The 'Response' being the twenty or so waiting customers hiding behind their clouds of tobacco smoke and newspapers. Approval or otherwise was signified by the amount of coughing or rustling of newspapers. But let no man interrupt the 'Chair's' incumbent. His discourse was sacrosanct.

The anecdotes emanating from the 'Chair' are legendary and would occupy a book in itself, but in order to illustrate such discussions I will mention a few. One gentleman, they all seemed to me as a small boy to be both huge and very old, sticks out

in my mind. On Fred's request, 'Next gentleman please', he would march up to the 'Chair' plonk himself down and with a theatrical gesture remove his hairpiece, (a wig in the 1950s!) and demand, 'a trim for me and a shampoo for the dog'. Pure delight. This request was invariably accompanied by an outburst of coughing and rustling of newsprint.

Fred, on occasions, was not above a gentle putting down of any over-pretentious client. There was an occasion where a youngish man of obvious aspirations, for he wore a white shirt and brown shoes, was, while on the 'chair', giving forth about what he did or did not do as an osteopath. Now in the 1950s, fringe medicine was unheard of, and it being extolled by such a person was extremely suspect within the shop's general strata of society. After a while the benevolent atmosphere in the shop changed subtly to one approaching exasperation. Fred, picking up the mood, quietly said, 'Then you are a bone manipulator'. 'No, an osteopath' came the reply. Fred pointed to another customer and said 'See that man, he is a street hygienist'. 'Oh!' said the incumbent, impressed. 'Yes' said Fred, 'He is a street sweeper and just to set the record straight you are being attended to by a tonsorial artist'. 'Well I never', said the victim, 'What's that?' 'I'm a barber', said Fred. That man never returned to the shop but as Fred sagely said, 'You cannot please everyone and sometimes a little wickedness is worth while'.

In the 1950s a barber's shop was probably the only place where men could buy contraceptives without undue embarrassment. Even so the subject was taboo, brand names were never mentioned, nor any direct request made. Fred, as ever aware to his customer's sensibilities would, on completion of the haircut, discreetly murmur, 'Anything for the weekend, sir?' This was completely understood. It was on one such occasion when a young man occupying the 'Chair' confessed that he was to be married that weekend. The haircut was completed and the aforementioned question asked. I remember the conversation as if it were yesterday 'Er, what will I need Fred?' 'How long are you on honeymoon?' 'Just Saturday and Sunday, I'm back at work come Monday'. There was a slight pause, Fred replied, 'I think ten packets of three would suffice sir'. There was a hysterical coughing and rustling of paper, but not a word spoken. Silence prevailed, the proprieties preserved. Merchandise and cash were duly exchanged; the young man left the shop. There was a pause, a collective splutter and then the place erupted, people rolling about with such mirth that I had never experienced, nor at that time could understand.

It was many years after Dad's retirement that my mother was mortified to be told that our annual holidays were funded by the profits obtained from Fred's oft-repeated request, 'Anything for the weekend, sir?'

By way of a postscript, Fred is now in his eighty-seventh year and is still active in mind and body. When he goes into town he is invariably stopped by one or other of the several generations of Cockerton folk who have passed through his shop, and are pleased to say 'I see you are alright, Fred'. As for me, now approaching sixty, some things have never changed; I still visit Dad for my monthly haircut. His skill and dexterous scissor work are still without compare.

Frank Butterfield (the barber's son)

A Beekeeping Saga

As a beekeeper for over fifty years and with the police, the Civic Centre and the museum all having my telephone number, I became unofficial pest officer for Darlington. For forty of these years I organized the setting up every spring of an Observation Beehive in the Darlington Museum. I was involved in removing swarms from a great variety of places; chimney pots seem to have an attraction for swarms.

My most interesting, amusing and sadly unsuccessful attempt to rescue a swarm from a chimney pot was on the end house of Beaconsfield Street, facing onto the grounds of the old maternity block of the Memorial Hospital.

The occupant of the house was a young mother with a two-year-old son whose father worked abroad. She phoned me saying she had bees coming down the chimney and into the dining room, despite the fireplace being occupied by a gas fire. She was scared not only for her own safety but mainly that of her son and could I help?

I visited her and she took me outside to show me the chimney pot from which I could see a lot of activity by bees. I looked at the height of the chimneystack and decided it was too high for a seventy-year-old to reach by ladders to deal with the bees. After reassuring her that I would return I went back home and phoned the fire brigade and explained the situation to the station officer. He regretted that only firemen were permitted up their turntable ladders. He did suggest that he could meet me at the site about 7.00 p.m., when he could come in a van with a fireman and one of their training smoke machines, and he was sure that the volume of smoke developed would drive the bees out. We met as arranged and station officer and fireman dismantled and removed the gas fire to allow the smoke machine to be fitted in its place. This was duly done but then the first mishap occurred. The machine did not work. The station officer blew his top at this failure and sent the fireman in the van to Bishop Auckland fire station, to collect their smoke machine.

In the meantime the young mother served us with tea and biscuits. It was after 11.00 p.m. when the van returned with the smoke machine and it was installed in the fireplace. The second mishap occurred when it also failed to function. I thought the station officer was going to need the services of his firemen as his anger exploded and he said all equipment, in both stations, must be tested in the morning.

He and the fireman then went into the grounds of the maternity hospital and gathered grass and leaves and set these on top of newspaper and started a fire which, indeed, created the necessary smoke. Now for mishap number three. Smoke was coming out of the wrong chimney. Bees were in the bedroom chimney pot, the fireplace of which had been bricked up. The time had now reached 1.00 a.m. so, after telling the young mother I would return during the day, the fireman and I went our separate ways.

In the morning I phoned Cllr Newton, who knew of my work with the Darlington Museum Observation Hive. I told him of the situation at Beaconsfield Street and asked whether he could arrange for the council snorkel wagon to lift me up. He agreed and phoned me later to say the wagon would be on site at 3.00 p.m. I was duly there, complete with veil (I never wear gloves) and a long-handled soup ladle, which I hoped would reach down to the bees and possibly bring out the queen. I also had some poison, in case I failed in this quest, and an old cloth to block the chimney pot. Now for mishap number four. The council wagon failed to take me to the necessary height. The driver phoned his boss who said he would arrange for the larger county snorkel wagon to come. This turned up at 4.00 p.m. By now there was quite a gathering of spectators including a borough engineer, a *Northern Echo* photographer and a bevy of nurses in the hospital grounds. I was lifted up, only to encounter mishap number five as the bees were too far down the chimney and I could not reach them. Sadly, I smothered them with poison and then blocked the chimney pot with the old cloth. Now for the final mishap, the snorkel driver was unable to lower me down. There was something wrong with the hydraulics so he shouted up to me to use the three levers in the box in which I was standing. Of course, these did not function either. I had visions of renewing my acquaintance with the firemen. The wagon driver started some dismantling and re-assembling and to the relief of all around I was lowered to ground level and greeted with clapping and cheers. A photograph of me up a height appeared in *The Northern Echo* the following morning!

A.E. Grey

CHAPTER 3
Buildings and Landmarks

No. 23, The first house to be built in Westbrook in 1861.

Westbrook, The Street I Left Behind

Westbrook is a tree-lined road just off High Northgate, which was for centuries the Great North Road. A village within the town, Westbrook lies about one and a half miles from the town centre. This privately owned and maintained row of Victorian Gothic houses, twenty-five in all overlooking the Cocker Beck, is certainly a rarity.

The lovely road dates from 1860 when it was built on Peases' garden. The houses were built for the better-class people who were connected with the Stockton and Darlington Railway and especially the locomotive works not far away in North Road. They are the only example of nineteenth-century middle-class housing in northern Darlington. Westbrook has escaped the ravages of developers over the years and at the beginning of the twenty-first century looks almost exactly as intended when designed at the height of the Victorian Gothic revival in the second half of the nineteenth century. Both as individual houses and as a group, these buildings are of special architectural and historic interest and the road has been designated a Conservation Area.

The first house was built in Westbrook in 1861. It was the double-fronted and detached Westbrook Cottage, which is now No. 23 and renamed Beechwood House.

The rear of the house rests on Station Road. It has a cottage where servants lived, and on the side is a yard which led on to the coal depots in their hey day and now leads on to Westbrook back street. Many of the original features of the house such as the doors, coving and skirting boards are still in place. The hall from the front door leads to an impressive staircase and continues round to a door which opens on to Station Road. Another door at the far end of the hall has the initials E, A and a larger R carved on both sides of its panels. The owner of the house in 1875 was E.A. Robinson. Over the years, the woodwork of the staircase had become neglected. The present owner, however, has had it splendidly restored, using the same kind of wood and in the original colour.

The large front garden with its magnificent beech trees has a centre path

Nos 8 and 8A Westbrook.

Nos 2 to 8 Westbrook, 1994. Number 8 Westbrook was the home of Bill and Betty Inns for forty-two years.

from the front gate to stone steps leading up to the front door of the house. This garden has a charming gazebo, which not only still sports its original ceiling painting but also 'goes round with the sun' just as it did in 1861. Mrs Lorraine Morgan has lived in this lovely house for twelve years and she has spent many hours bringing it back to its Victorian glory.

An old street directory shows that in 1871 The Villa, No. 8 Westbrook, was a private boarding school for boys. Listed as living there were Mr Christopher Jackson, Mr Henry Mason the assistant master, Isabella Hodgson, Christopher, Ethel and Eleanor Walton, Ann Wilson the housemaid, Elizabeth Nelson the nursemaid and seventeen boys. After 1881 No. 8 became a family home again. One of the earliest built in Westbrook it was a large

house overlooking beautiful gardens and Cocker Beck.

The four-storey residence had a basement with kitchens and living quarters for the staff, whose bedrooms were on the top floor. The basement as a whole was very large and had its own front entrance with steps leading down to its door. One of the kitchens had a large iron fireplace, coal oven and an iron boiler that heated water for the entire house. Away from the basement the house had two large sitting rooms, large dining rooms, cloakroom, hall with a winding staircase leading off to the bathroom with toilet, two linen cupboards and ten bedrooms. There were stables and outbuildings, not to mention a cottage in grounds at the side of the house for a groom or handyman. Of course, a wealthy family lived here. They went everywhere in their pony and trap.

The old-fashioned garden of No. 12.

In 1897 this enormous place was split into two lovely houses with additions being built on either side. What a splendid job was made of it. Today, no one can tell that the two houses were once one. The two homes remain as they were a century ago retaining all the main features. They are built of the same white brick as Darlington's old town hall, town clock, indoor market and other Victorian buildings, most notably those built for the Pease dynasty of Quaker entrepreneurs. In 1970, there was a move by the council to place architectural value preservation orders on the two houses but demolition being carried out behind them apparently caused a change of plan.

Next we come to No. 12 Westbrook which was built in 1865. This house was bought by a master mariner, Captain King, in 1900 and for the last century generations of the King family have lived here. It was in this house that during the Second World War an incendiary bullet from a German aircraft hit a wall before lodging itself in an old-fashioned door sneck without doing any real damage. No. 12 has six bedrooms, sitting room, dining room, a kitchen with its original features and a self-contained basement. There is a most notable wrought-iron veranda outside a front bedroom and much else in the house is also original. Across Westbrook Road beside the stream is the house's lovely old-fashioned garden, with flowering trees and a pond, which is home to frogs and newts.

Nos 17 and 18 Westbrook are six-bedroom houses. No. 17 has been owned for sixteen years by Mr John Curry, a schoolteacher, and his wife Jean, who derive a lot of pleasure from the bay-windowed sitting room looking over the front garden. An advertisement in the *Darlington and Stockton Times* in 1875 tells us that in No. 18 all that space was used to prepare young ladies for university – it was a private school for girls and called Westbrook House. In the days of the Stockton and Darlington Railway it seems that this town was quite a centre for education, an 'Athens of the North' as some people dubbed it.

In 1972 Mr Dorian Pigg, who still lives behind the original front door today, bought No. 18. Indeed, all interior doors and coving are also original. Next to the main kitchen, what began life as a coach house is now a study. There is a second kitchen which was once used by the servants of the house. The sitting room bay window looks on to the front garden and across Westbrook Road is another lovely garden, which leads down to Cocker Beck and a private footbridge.

At No. 19, one half of a semi-detached pair built in 1880; long-time residents were Frank Holmes, his wife and their two daughters. He was born in Westbrook and his parents once lived in No. 18, first moving into the road in the late nineteenth century. When he died in 1991 his daughters sold the house. The new owner converted a cellar into a basement room, which includes a door opening on to steps leading up to the front garden. Since then, the house has changed hands again, and it is an owner-occupier whose family have the pleasure of their second garden over the road by the beck, with its flowers, fruit trees and an attractive old pond.

The adjoining No. 20 is another house whose exterior and, indeed, interior have remained virtually unchanged for well over a century. As if a long garden on the other side of the road is not enough, this house also boasts a paddock reached by its private footbridge over the Cocker Beck. To go across into this extra green space is like entering another world. Pigeon lofts belonging to the late husband of Mrs Rhoda Robinson, who has lived in the house for forty-six years, can be found in the paddock. Arthur Robinson was well known in the pigeon world and details of his prize-winning career were often to be found in the *Evening Despatch*, *Northern Echo* and the fanciers' magazines.

The last two houses to be built in Westbrook were Nos 24 and 25. These two large three-storey semi-detached houses were built in the late nineteenth century. They back on to Station Road and their fronts overlook the gardens, Cocker Beck and Westbrook Road. There are small front gardens with a long flight of stone steps up to the front doors. All work was completed in Westbrook by 1896.

The street behind Westbrook led up to the coal yards and the coal-drops which have links with the Stockton and Darlington Railway and North Road station. Coal trucks ran from the station and came down the middle of Station Road to the coal-drops. Coal would be tipped, via the drops, into the coal yards for purchase by the merchants. Some of the coal-drops survive; three garages on what is now the back street to Westbrook still have them inside. Wells were once in most of the backyards and in the gardens across from Westbrook Road. Most of these have now disappeared, but in the early days they provided the Victorians with their drinking water.

School pupils sketching Nos 8 and 8A Westbrook, 1997.

Turn the corner at No. 25 Westbrook and just ahead is the wrought-iron gate where the private road ends. As one walks back through Westbrook it makes one proud to know that there is a street such as this in Darlington, which has not been spoiled by development. Education establishments in Darlington, Aycliffe and other neighbouring towns often send pupils to study and sketch these Victorian houses. This elegant street of considerable historical interest should never be interfered with; a full preservation order ought years ago to have been placed on this unique piece of Victoriana.

As we stroll back down the road, between front gardens and the beck side flowers, we should keep a watch out for woodpeckers, owls, kingfishers and other uncommon birds often seen in this quiet nineteenth-century byway. We reach the narrow entrance and pass back through into High Northgate and the noise and hustle of a less genteel millennium.

Betty Inns
The author was granted permission by the
residents of Westbrook to use their names.

St Andrew's Church, Haughton-le-Skerne

A Brief History

St Andrew's church is one of the most ancient and beautiful churches in the North of England. It is essentially Norman, probably dating back to 1125, but the evidence of the Saxon relics which are now embedded in the church walls prove that there has been a church on this site dating back to Saxon times. Following the missions from Lindisfarne, most of Northumbria was Christian by the middle of the seventh century, and the site of St Andrew's church, built on a mound cut out by the River Skerne, is most likely to have had a church from the earliest times.

Styr, son of Ulf, was said to have bestowed Haughton, or *Halhtune*, to the Episcopal See of Durham 'for St Cuthbert', at the beginning of the eleventh century. The original Saxon church was believed to have been destroyed by William the Conqueror's army during the 'Harrowing of the North' in 1068. The nave is the oldest part of the building now, dating back to the late eleventh or early twelfth century, and the chancel was added in about 1175.

On entering the porch, the visitor passes a Saxon cross and other Saxon relics embedded in the walls (p. 52). These were discovered at the time of the major reconstruction work of 1895 when part of a wall had to be pulled down. There are also some crusader coffin lids, medieval grave covers. They are inscribed with a sword (for a man) and shears and a key (for a woman). The original porch, from early times until the middle of the nineteenth century, was where much civil business was transacted. Notices were displayed and marriage banns published.

The door into the church is Norman, and immediately opposite is the blocked-up north door. Here, part of a Saxon cross is displayed, possibly the original which stood in the churchyard. There are some other interesting stones, which may be of Scandinavian (Viking) origin, dating to the first half of the tenth century. There is a frieze that depicts a wild boar hunt (p. 53).

Towards the baptistry, embedded in the North wall, are more stones and figures (p. 53). These were discovered at the time of the reconstruction. The red stone at the base on the right is believed to date back to AD 700 and there is also a shaft of a Saxon cross.

Two views of St Andrew's church, Haughton-le-Skerne.

Turning from the nave to the west, there is the tower with the baptismal font. The tower was a later addition, built around 1175, and rebuilt in the thirteenth century. The door is not in line with the centre of the tower wall, but with the centre of the nave. A fragment of one of the original pillars at either side of the original door can be found in the South Transept. It is cut into hollows, presumably by the sharpening of swords and weapons at the church door. (p. 53) The tower houses three bells. One of the bells was cast well before 1550, and the other two in 1663 and 1664 respectively, by Samuel Smith of York. The earliest bell is known as the Alphabet Bell. It may be the sole remaining one of its type and still bears some letters of the alphabet engraved in reverse.

Prior to the reconstruction of 1895, the base of the tower was the entrance to the nave, (the west door being the main

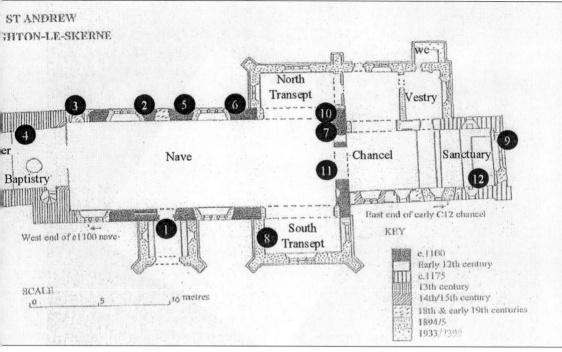

ST ANDREW
HIGHTON-LE-SKERNE

North Transept

WC

Vestry

Nave

Chancel

Sanctuary

Baptistry

West end of c1100 nave

East end of early C12 chancel

South Transept

KEY

c.1100
Early 12th century
c.1175
13th century
14th/15th century
18th & early 19th centuries
1894/5
1933/1989

SCALE
0   5   10 metres

Below: *A Saxon cross embedded in the porch walls.*

Above: *Diagram of St Andrew's church.*

entrance to the church), and the Gallery stairs. Nothing is now visible of the gallery, which was erected in 1725, but there is a stone slab now resting on the ledge of the west window of the south wall of the nave, which bears the initials of the church wardens at the time of its installation. It was erected in the time of Rector Joseph Butler, presumably because more accommodation was needed for the growing congregation (there were no transepts at that time). The gallery was further extended, but was removed in 1894.

In 1895 the base of the tower was cleared to allow for the font, and the church wardens' seats were taken to the back of the church. The shaft of the font is believed to be the twelfth or early thirteenth century, and is made of Frosterley marble. The original bowl cracked as a result of the water

Stones and figures found during the reconstruction of the church.

Stones embedded in the walls, possibly of Scandinavian origin and a frieze depicting a wild boar hunt.

freezing in the bowl over many winters and so was replaced at the time of the reconstruction work. Following legislation in the thirteenth century requiring all fonts to be kept locked; Holy Water was being stolen and a canopy was installed. The present one dates to Jacobean times (p. 54)

Under the carpet of the baptistry in front of the font, there are two stone slabs. The first commemorates the memory of M. William Harrison ('late of Barmpton. A man whose benevolence and humble disposition gained him universal esteem: he lived respected and died lamented 1 Dec 1782. Aged 67'). The other commemorates Elizabeth Nanton, Prioress of Neasham. The inscription reads, 'Under ys to laith D am Elsabeth Nanton Proires of the soul Jhu have merci' which translates as 'under this stone lies Dame

Fragment of a pillar, now located in the South Transept.

The font canopy dating from the Jacobean period.

Elizabeth Nanton Prioress, of the soul Jesus have mercy.' Elizabeth Nanton is believed to have been the last Prioress of Neasham in 1489. It is not known for certain why she was buried at Haughton. There is nothing remaining of Neasham Abbey, and the stone could have been brought from there to Haughton church. There had been connections between the two earlier in the century when, in 1436, Richard Pennymaster, Rector of Haughton-le-Skerne, and the Abbot of Byland were appointed to conduct a visitation of the nunnery, and Elizabeth Nanton's earlier predecessor was left with many instructions as to the conduct of the nunnery, under pain

of deprivation of her office. Elizabeth Nanton was not tainted in any way as Prioress. It is suggested that she may have been buried at Haughton because at the time of her death she was living at Sadberge.

Turning from the tower, facing towards the chancel, the picture is that of a seventeenth-century church with its stained oak gated pews and wall panels, encompassed within the Norman church walls. The church is now in cruciform shape. St Andrews church was altered in the late nineteenth century to reflect the changing doctrine and theology of the time. The Eucharist became the focal point of worship.

The pews and woodwork date from the seventeenth century. The pews in the nave, the dado in the nave and the chancel, the two pulpits, the communion rail, the altar beneath the frontal and the sanctuary chairs are Jacobean, and are known as 'Cosin's woodwork'. Cosin was rector of Brancepth in 1626, and after the Commonwealth, Bishop of Durham. Most of the woodwork belongs to the early restoration work of Bishop Neil and Cosin. The font canopy is slightly later, believed to be 1662. Other examples of 'Cosin's woodwork' can be found in the chapel at Auckland Castle, in Durham Cathedral and Sedgefield, Ryton and Easington parish churches. We are grateful to graffiti artists for leaving us with some evidence of dating: a shelf in a pew has a date carved 1639, and behind the rector's stall there are two cockerels and the date 1649.

Walking up the aisle, on the north wall are placed two hatchments. The word 'hatchment' is derived from the language of Heraldry from the two words 'funeral' and 'achievements'. The hatchments accompanied the body to the graveside and

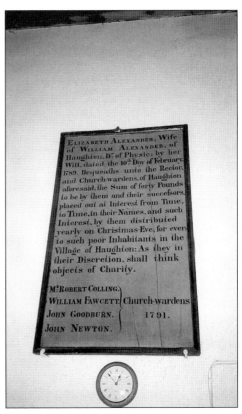

ELIZABETH ALEXANDER, Wife
of WILLIAM ALEXANDER, of
Haughton, D.r of Physic; by her
Will, dated the 10.th Day of February,
1789. Bequeaths unto the Rector,
and Church-wardens, of Haughton
aforesaid, the Sum of forty Pounds
to be by them and their successors,
placed out at Interest from Time,
to Time, in their Names, and such
Interest, by them distributed
yearly on Christmas-Eve, for ever
to such poor Inhabitants in the
Village of Haughton: As they in
their Discretion, shall think
objects of Charity.

M.r ROBERT COLLING.
WILLIAM FAWCETT Church-wardens
JOHN GOODBURN. 1791.
JOHN NEWTON.

The portrait and benefaction of Mrs Alexander located in the upper vestry.

were afterwards placed in the church. One of the hatchments bears the arms of the Alexander family, and the other of the Byron family. The Hon. Richard Byron was rector 1795-1811, and was the youngest son of the 4th Lord Byron. Mrs Alexander was a benefactress of the parish whose charity was distributed to widows every Christmas. Her benefaction and portrait are in the upper vestry.

The royal coat of arms of George II hangs between the two hatchments. Bishop Butler was rector from 1721-1725 and was Clerk of the Closet to King George II, so entitled to display the royal coat of arms in church. The coat of arms, however, is not of George II as the inscription suggests, but the Stuart coat

of arms. Two reasons have been suggested for this anomaly. Firstly, the church already had a coat of arms and it saved expense just to add the name of George II. Secondly, Haughton-le-Skerne was well known for its Jacobite sympathies and this was therefore a snub to the Hanoverians.

Looking from the nave to the altar, there are two arches, one on top of the other. The lower arch is Norman. The Gothic chancel arch with the crucifix was installed when the pitched roof was added, the crucifix being given in memory of a former rector, Revd J.C. Fellowes. At the chancel arch are four brasses, all commemorating the same family. They show a woman with her two babies. The woman is Dorothy Parkinson

The altar with two arches above it, the higher is a Gothic arch and below it a Norman arch.

who died after giving birth to twins, who also died. The children are shown wearing 'chrisom' clothes, indicating they would have died within a month of baptism. One inscription plaque reads 'Dorothy, Daughter of Richard Cholmeley Esquire, the third sonne to Sir Richard Chomeley, Knight, late of Robert Parkinson of Whessey, Gentleman, departed this life the Nineteenth day of Julye 1592 and lyeth buryed neare this place, with hir twoe twines, Richard Parkinson and Marmaduke Parkinson, sonnes of the said Robert and Dorothy.'

The history of the church, the changing patterns of worship and the development of doctrine can be seen in the different styles of windows. At the east end of the chancel the height of the flat roof is visible in the remains of the window arch. The present window was installed in 1895. Before this, the window had three single lights. In the north and south sides of the chancel and sanctuary are three of the original early Norman narrow windows, with rounded tops. The windows in St Andrew's church are from four different periods: the Norman ones in the chancel, the early English one in the chancel, which dates from about 1370, the perpendicular window in the tower, dating from about 1450, and the Victorian Gothic windows in the remainder of the church, dating from the end of the nineteenth century.

On the north side of the chancel arch is the 'squint'. The original reason for a squint was to enable a priest who was administering the Host at Mass to be able to see another priest elsewhere in the church doing the same, in order for the Host to be celebrated at exactly the same time. It is uncertain whether this is the original purpose for the squint in St Andrew's

The height of the original flat roof is visible in the remains of this window arch.

church. It may have been installed for the rector to have a view of his congregation during the service; the clergy stalls originally facing the altar. Alternatively it may have been to allow the parishioners a better view of the altar.

To the south side of the chancel arch, behind the pulpit, is a recess, which still retains some of its original fresco painting. This recess may well have housed a statue of the Virgin Mary. The fresco painting predates the Reformation. Prior to this time, the church may well have had frescoes painted on all the walls of the nave and chancel, but there are none remaining. Walking up the chancel, to the south side behind the sanctuary chair is a blocked-up

The church organ dating from 1899.

St Andrew's church is a living place of worship serving the community of this part of Darlington. In this millennium (2000) the building will be further enhanced to aid worship and to reach out to the community.

Bryan Robson and Philippa Sinclair

Mickleton Gets An Institute

Twenty-odd miles into Darlington's rural hinterland lies the Teesdale village of Mickleton. It's lain there a long time. Forty years before Columbus discovered America, Edward Raine and two Dent brothers were fined by Lord Fitzhugh for grazing their sheep in his deer forests. Fourteen generations of those Dents have lived in Mickleton since the 1500s, one strand in fact living in the same house, High Green, from 1752 until 1986 when Tom Dent, last of the male line in Mickleton, died. Similarly, the Raine family farmed continuously at West Pasture from 1607 until 1907; and Ronnie, the family's last representative in the village, survived almost until the year 2000. Generations of Parkins, Atkinsons, Collinsons, Bainbridges, Waltons, Dowsons and others can also be found in parish records down the years, all direct forebears of families still traceable in Mickleton today. Mickleton's Village Hall, newly built in 1993, traces its beginnings – more modestly – to the closing days of Queen Victoria's reign.

On 13 September 1895, the vicar killed himself. The Revd William Bell was found drowned in the Lune, the shallow river which still tumbles through the steep wood opposite the vicarage. There had to be an inquest. The elderly Revd Bell had been a much-loved and active vicar for thirty years

fourteenth century 'low-side' window. Its purpose may have been for excommunicates and lepers to be able to observe Mass without coming into physical contact with those in the church. Alternatively, there may have been a doorway in this position.

The organ in the chancel dates from 1899. The original organ was built by George Hoggett of Darlington and was installed in the gallery in 1841. Following the major readjustment work at the end of the nineteenth century, an organ chamber was created in the chancel, and the present organ, built by Forster and Andrews of Hull, was installed at a total cost of £370. Above the rector's stall is the coat of arms of the Royal School of Church Music.

but, as his housekeeper told the Barnard Castle Court, he had been partially paralysed for the last four years of his life and, not surprisingly, had been depressed. Sensibly, most villagers assumed he had ended his own life. However, the Coroner's view was inevitably influenced by wider society's attitudes at that time. Suicide was a criminal offence. To recognize that a gentleman of the cloth had committed such an act, would not look well. Worse, it would exclude the Revd Bell from burial in his own churchyard. Naturally, the Coroner didn't spell this out. But he did 'advise' the jury, whereupon they recorded the simple verdict 'Found Drowned'.

The Revd Bell's death created a vacancy. Coming as it did at a time of some social unease in the countryside, the choice of a new vicar had consequences for the village, which still have their effects today. In fact, the two incumbents following the Revd

Bell's death chronicle between them the peak, then a slow decline, of the status of the Church of England country vicar over the years surrounding Queen Victoria's death.

A gift – with a view?

The Revd George Ramsden became the new vicar in 1895. Within two years, he had made two most generous gifts to the village — the church of St Mary Magdalene (known thereafter as 'the mission church'), and the Church Institute next to it.

The Revd Ramsden's generosity was impressive. His halo is therefore secure. But the Church of England would not have achieved the position it did during those Victorian times, had its clergy not been shrewd as well as generous. The Revd Ramsden's gifts were sallies in a genteel struggle for souls, then going on in the village. He was also surely influenced, as a

The original mission church and institute in Mickleton. Inset: Benefactor, the Revd Ramsden.

local establishment figure, by signs of unrest then threatening village calm and order.

Competition for souls was clearly a factor. The Wesleyan Methodists had built a brand new church only five years earlier on Low Side – almost next door to where Revd Ramsden now chose to build his mission church. The Primitive Methodists too had a chapel and theirs was equally close, at Bank Top. Potential Methodists thus had two chapels to tempt them, both in the middle of the village. Church of England 'supporters' however, had to trudge all the way to Laithkirk, a hilltop church a mile outside the village.

As to social unrest, life for villagers certainly wasn't easy. Quarrying and lead mining was the life's work of most men. Mark Anderson, grandfather of current resident Floyd Anderson, left school aged eleven in 1881 and walked five miles each way every day from neighbouring Newbiggin, to work at Mickleton's Bail Hill Quarry (now the home of Teesdale Gun Club). Ronnie Raine's grandfather, a lead-miner, would walk more miles and sleep in workmens' huts all week because his work at Weardale Mine was too far to walk daily. The other main employment was for the 'navvies' building the Grassholme reservoir; they camped full time on site. Certain small items in the Teesdale *Mercury* around Christmas 1892 provide a flavour of the atmosphere of the times: an atmosphere which might well have prompted the Mickleton 'establishment', including its new vicar, to decide that the ordinary villagers needed some attention.

One such item reported a Christmas sale of work at the Primitive Methodist chapel, where a pie supper disappeared with marvellous rapidity, which speaks well for ladies of Mickleton as pie bakers. However, we are sorry to say the people lasted longer than the pies, some having to be turned away hungry.

Another item reported a magic lantern lecture at the Wesleyan chapel on 'Scenes of London': 'The lecturer, a London gentleman, introduced sharp witticisms, which were heartily appreciated.' However, 'the bad boy element was rather strong, trying to enliven the proceedings by thinking aloud'. Finally, 'A Ratepayer' wrote the following anxious letter to the *Mercury*. Was his letter prompted by the 'thinking aloud' of the pie-hungry bad boy elements?

Sir,

Will you allow me to suggest a few thoughts in respect to the village of Mickleton? We are making improvements in regard to sewerage which will, I have no doubt, be a benefit to the health of the village. We have a population of about 600 and the quarries employ all the young men. There is no place to draw to these winter evenings but the public house. I think there ought to be something done to provide them with a reading room, for resort, after their day's work is done. If we want to win them to sobriety and intelligence, and make them right-thinking men, let us help them in the right direction. I think the proprietors of our surrounding village ought to take the first step and I have no doubt the poorer classes will help with their share. I am certain if we had something done for them, it would be one great step towards improving, both socially and spiritually, the inhabitants of our village.

A Ratepayer

All this is not to suggest that Mickleton saw scenes of riot and unrest in the 1890s, but the conditions of life villagers had to lead was unsettling enough to prompt Mickleton's 'proprietors' to think that something – a 'sober meeting place'? – should be provided. The Revd Ramsden's appointment in 1895 therefore came at a time when opinion was ripe to provide 'something for the masses'.

There was opposition though. Some felt any such provision should be independent of the church. The Parish Council Minutes of 2 May 1896 recorded a vote to erect 'by public subscription a Reading Room for the benefit of the Public of Mickleton.' A Mr Langstaff of Greengates offered the council some land for the purpose, at a rent of sixpence a year. Given this, the councillors decided in August 'to canvass the Township and ascertain if the Ratepayers are in favour of a Reading Room', by public subscription if possible. The Township was in favour. But the public subscriptions didn't flow. 'A concert in aid of a Village Reading Room' produced only £4 15s 6d. That wasn't going to build a Reading Room, even if Mr Langstaff's offer was taken up.

It was then, perhaps, that the Revd Ramsden saw his opportunity, both to help out the 'proprietors' and also to influence a few souls in his Church's direction. He had already built his Mission church. Whatever his motives, he now came to the rescue with his donation of a 'sober meeting place' on the plot of land next to his church.

It was thus that Mickleton's village hall lost the secular independence which the parish councillors had hoped for, and became instead 'The Church Institute' – provided, as the Deeds put it, 'for ever for the benefit of the persons residing...being members of or connected with the Established Church of England'. The villagers certainly appreciated the Institute and quickly made full use of it. But feelings

over such matters never entirely disappear. No-one was ever refused its use: but even sixty years later, as recalled by John Walton, a church member then active in running the Institute, 'Some villagers still regarded the Institute as not theirs – it was the Church's'.

The Church Institute was finished and opened in December 1897, a year or so after the Mission church. In its first year, the Institute contributed £2 6s 8d to parish church funds. It was already in use nearly a year before the Deeds were signed – a practice which would not have pleased conveyancing solicitors today! Like the church, the Institute was built quickly and with economy in mind. Indeed, the two buildings were revolutionary for their time for they were prefabricated and made of corrugated iron.

The vicar's building – the lord's land

Like much of Mickleton, the buildings occupied land owned by Lord Strathmore, land that is still owned by that family. The lease was from 'The Right Hon. Claude, Earl of Strathmore & Kinghorne and Baron Bowes of Streatlam Castle, tenant for life in the Wemmergill Settled Estates, to The Revd George Ramsden, Clerk & Incumbent of the Parish of Laithkirk in the County of York...' Two church officials and His Lordship's agent were also named. The earl's advisers took care not to let his generosity run away with him: the conveyance reserved rights to the earl, his agents and workmen 'to mines and minerals and underground passages and access necessary for the winning, working and carrying away of minerals'. This reflects the substantial lead mining industry which characterized Teesdale at that time. Fortunately for the foundations of the buildings, no underground discoveries were subsequently made to tempt the earl to exercise those rights.

Church giving – and withholding

After ten years, the Revd Ramsden left. He was succeeded in 1905 by the Revd Francis Holmes, a Cambridge University graduate. Vestry accounts suggest a growing prosperity in the parish, plus a new vicar keen to favour worthy causes. Given that a man's weekly wage was little more than one pound a week, the vestry's donations were quite substantial. 'Outside world' events must also have had their influence: revolution was stirring in Russia; women in London were demanding the vote; and Parliament had just 'welcomed' its first Labour MPs. In 1905, £10 13s 10d went solely to church charities – the Women's Home Missionary Association; the Diocesan Societies; The Society for the Propagation of the Gospel; and 1s 10d for the ladies of the East Grinstead Sisterhood. 1906 saw greater but more 'social' generosity. A total of £14 16s 2d went to causes ranging from the British and Foreign Bible Society to the Navvy Mission (for the encamped Grassholme labourers) and The Sick and Needy. In 1908 however, the vestry decided to look to its own needs: specifically, to end its dependence on a hired organ and buy its own. They raised the necessary £250 in only two years, a considerable achievement. But the investment was clearly a good one, for that organ is still in fine voice and regular use in Laithkirk church today.

The collapse of the lead mines

Just as the Church was dispensing this charity, the needs of the village itself suddenly became dire. The London Lead Company, in 1905, finally closed all its mines and smelting mills in Teesdale. The effects on employment can be imagined. Mickleton was especially hard hit.

The company's policy was to behave decently as long as it could: they eased the hardship in Eggleston and Middleton by distributing flour. But for some reason Mickleton was overlooked — perhaps because at that time Mickleton was beyond the county boundary, in Yorkshire. In consequence, many Mickleton families abandoned their homes and left the area, some even left the country. Some found work in the coal mine at Woodlands, pushing their heavy bikes seven miles uphill before starting work – and cycling home again on winter nights, one eye-witness recounted, with clothes, moustaches and eyebrows frozen. Villagers turned over every patch of spare land they could find, to grow potatoes. These vegetable passports to survival afterwards earned the villagers the nickname 'Mickleton Tatey Kites'. It is an historic episode still present in the collective memory, for there is a section in today's village hall called the Tatey Kites Junior Youth Club.

The hard times must also have hit the Revd Holmes, notwithstanding his earlier concern for the needy elsewhere. Less wealthy than George Ramsden, his plight was so severe that he felt obliged, in November 1909, to broadcast the facts in the Teesdale *Mercury*. After pointing out bitterly that the parish's large acreage had been constituted in 1844 with a fixed yearly stipend of £100 'solely for the convenience of the then rector of Romaldkirk', he complained that he was still expected to do his job, sixty-five years later, on a stipend of only £13 10s 0d more. His *Mercury* letter went on to appeal for 'the sum of £150 for which I am personally responsible, for debts on four schools and churches and Assistant Curates Fund; and such capital sum as will ensure, if not to me, at least to my successors, a "living wage". I would gladly furnish all the facts, figures and circumstances of the situation (which are not very creditable to the

"Establishment" as such). I have, during the last four-and-a-half years appealed to those on whom we might be supposed to have some sort of claim for financial aid but without very much success, and those who know anything of the true inwardness of a country parson's life will readily understand that such a parish as this quite easily absorbs the greater part of any private means the parson happens to have.

The Revd Holmes' cry for help did not soften the 'establishment' towards him. Indeed, his public washing of ecclesiastical linen doubtless antagonised them; and small-town prejudice about his Cambridge BA might also have contributed. Thus, lacking response to his cry, he struggled on for nineteen months more, and then resigned. A photograph of the Revd Holmes' farewell presentation shows him, slouching, hands in pockets, on the stage of the Institute, addressing his few words of thanks to a very unsmiling group of local dignitaries.

Overhead flies the banner WELCOME TO ALL UNITY IS STRENGTH.

Three years later, the world was at war. But the Institute, product of his predecessor and the prevailing social situation, was by now the well-established centre of Mickleton's daily life.

Its spirit lives on. In 1990, the Church Institute was condemned. To replace Revd Ramsden's 1897 gift of £327 16s 1d, villagers now had to raise £140,000. Undaunted, within three years they had created a fine new stone-built hall. The building won numerous awards, even inspired other villages. But its real value shows in its almost daily occupation since its formal opening – by today's Lord Strathmore – in 1994.

S. Walinets

The leaving ceremony and presentation to Revd Holmes, July 1911.

Mickleton Village Hall, 2001.

The Hell's Kettles Of Darlington

There are many mysterious happenings and events in the history of Darlington but one of the main centres of attraction when it comes to mysteries is our famous 'Hell's Kettles'. So what is this mystery all about?

On the road to Croft from Darlington, and about half a mile from Hurworth Place, on the left hand side of the road as it sweeps round in an arc, you will see in the hedgerow, a stile. Going through this stile, and just a few yards ahead of you, there are two pools, or ponds of water. These are the remains of what was once three pools and these are the 'Hell's Kettles'. Let us begin with from where and when these pools came.

Our story begins in 1179, not long before the building of our church of St Cuthbert in the town centre. In this year, says *Brampton's Chronicle*, about Christmas a marvellous event occurred. News had come that a great wonder had chanced at a place called Oxenhale within the Lordship of Darlington, in which place a part of the earth lifted itself up on height in appearance of a mighty tower and so it remained from nine o'clock in the morning until the eventide. It then fell down with a horrible noise and all in this district were in great fear. The piece of earth that fell was swallowed up leaving a great deep pit in the place as was to be seen many years after.

It would appear that what was being described in very old English style was what we would call today a small earthquake that left a large hole in the ground. Perhaps the erosion of

THE OTHER HELLS KETTLE - CROFT ROAD

One of the Hell's Kettles near Croft Road.

Northgate in the late 1800s.

underground limestone and the presence of gas, which ignited under pressure, caused this quake. Whatever the cause, the result was a huge hole that gradually filled up with water released from an underground spring by the explosion.

Perhaps over the next few hundred years this large pit became divided into three, or even more pools, but only three have ever been mentioned. They are all probably fed from the same spring and have no connection with the nearby River Tees, as when the Tees is in flood the 'Kettles' remain the same. It is not that many years ago that the smallest pool was filled in to leave just the two surviving ones that you can see today.

Over the years many wonderful scary stories have been associated with these pools. One such story was of a luckless farmer who had accidentally driven his horse and cart into the larger pool and was swallowed up and drowned. It was said that when the day was quiet and

windless you could see the horse and cart shimmering way down below the surface. There were and still are a multitude of similar stories of ghostly apparitions, howling animals and the like. To me the intention is clear – to keep the younger children away from the place by sheer fear. It is a dangerous area to a non-swimmer and the water can get very cold indeed. However, here they are and here they will remain, 'The Hell's Kettles' of Darlington.

Ron Watson

Darlington's Stones

Bulmer's Stone is pictured (p. 66) in the late 1800s outside weavers' cottages on Northgate. This glacial erratic is the oldest landmark in Darlington and inherited its name from William Bulmer, the town crier. He would stand on the stone to read the news. The stone now stands outside the council offices on the corner of Northgate and Gladstone Street. This building was originally the town's Technical College and is built on the site of the weavers' cottages.

The life of W.T. Stead is commemorated by the Tethering Stone outside Darlington's Library. W.T. Stead was once editor of *The Northern Echo* and he would tether his pony to this boulder while at his office. Stead is known to have drowned on the *Titanic* in 1912.

Claire Bulman

W.T Stead's Tethering Stone outside Darlington Library.

Bulmer's Stone in its present location in Northgate.

CHAPTER 4

Railways, Industry and Trolleybuses

Locomotion No. 1, *Bank Top station. (Copyright*, The Northern Echo)

Have You Got A Light?

Robert Metcalf was a navvy, a rare breed of men, who first built the canals and then the railways. Some called them 'despicable' because of their lifestyle – hard working and hard drinking. They travelled and had no local loyalty, living as they pleased. Robert

Repainted Locomotion No. 1, 1961. (*Copyright*, The Northern Echo)

however was different. Although he was uneducated, he did become literate, but his most important task, while still a young man, may have changed the course of history.

In 1822 Robert gained employment as a navvy on the planned Stockton and Darlington Railway, in the first place at Earlynook. He stayed there for a while, until a distant relative told him there was work at Heighington, and encouraged Robert to go there, as he was the foreman.

It was whilst working on the Heighington section that a landslip occurred, trapping Robert, breaking both his legs and collarbone. The company doctor

(Fothergill) attended Robert, and it was his care that helped ensure a reasonable recovery for him. When Robert returned to the railway cutting workings he was not fit enough to go back to his old job. This problem, however, solved another problem. Robert's cousin had to work on the railway workings, as well as try to supervise the men, and he found he could not do both. At the same time, Robert was using his, so far, latent management skills, and could see where the inefficiencies were, and where advantage was being taken of his cousin. Robert discussed this with his cousin, who said the men were good for nothing, and would Robert help to supervise the men.

Robert agreed, but he knew he would have to stamp his authority on the men immediately. One of the navvies was a particularly obnoxious man, who, when he was not working, was threatening and abusive. Ensuring the men could see what was happening, Robert called the obnoxious man across, and paid him off, telling him that the company did not need men like him! The wages were paid fortnightly, and with Robert in charge, cajoling and pushing, the men were clearing 2,000 yards a fortnight.

On 27 September 1825, when the railway line was finished, Robert and his co-workers were at Heighington awaiting the arrival of *Locomotion No. 1*. The engine arrived, and was placed on the line, the boiler was filled with water, and the firebox was laid with wood, coal and oakum (untwined rope soaked in tar). Everything was set, but the fallibility of man showed itself. Nobody had the foresight to bring any means of lighting the fire! While everyone was standing around, looking embarrassed, John Taylor was sent to Aycliffe to get a lantern. After Taylor had gone, Robert decided to have a smoke of his pipe. He lit it with his pipe glass, and then, inspired, he asked George Stephenson if he could try and light the fire with his pipe glass. This was agreed, the fire was started, and *Locomotion No. 1* began making steam.

We cannot be sure that John Taylor would have got back with a lantern, and thus, if Robert had not had his pipe glass, *Locomotion No. 1* may not have run and the transport history of Great Britain may have been changed.

When the engine had been started, all the navvies climbed into eight wagons which were attached to *Locomotion No. 1*. The train went to North Road, Darlington, where the navvies disembarked and went to the Three Tuns Inn for a celebratory meal.

And the rest, as they say, is history!

Barry Ranns

A Circle of Life at North Road Station

When youth has long gone, the preservation of a place filled with happy childhood memories seems nothing less than a dream come true. At Darlington's North Road station, now both a station and railway museum, that dream has become joyful reality. It is pure nostalgia to stand once more on the platform where long ago, an excited schoolboy watched eagerly for the steam train, which was transport to the delights of summer holidays in Teesdale.

Such romantic reverie has compelling appeal, but the hard facts of history show that North Road's pre-eminent place in railway heritage has been achieved by survival against the enemies of war and stringent business economics. That I have lived with North Road through its 'dark decades' of the twentieth century is a matter that I will take care to record as an accompaniment to historical fact. The writing of such a tribute will never be less than a labour of love.

My first sight of North Road station, or rather, its environs, was in 1937. My father had moved from the West Midlands to take up employment with the Whessoe Engineering Company in Darlington. We moved to a house in the Pierremont district and I was soon enrolled as a pupil at Corporation Road elementary school, which I quickly learned, was near North Road station.

North Road Railway Museum. (Copyright, Ray Allison)

I travelled to school on Darlington's trolley buses fondly known by a generation who remembered the town's earlier trams as 'the trackless'. I waited for the 'trollies' in their attractive blue cream livery at a bus stop in Hopetown Lane behind Westbrook Villas. I was pleased to find that across the road behind a high retaining wall were the sidings adjoining North Road railway station. I had been given a Hornby train set for my seventh birthday earlier that year and now, on every single school day I could see real life versions of the wagons that my clockwork engine hauled round a simple circular track.

At Corporation Road school I soon learned that Darlington was the 'home of railways'. Although George Stephenson had developed steam locomotives to haul wagons of coal on colliery sites, the first use of steam power on a public railway with scheduled service occurred when the Stockton and Darlington Railway opened in 1825. The Darlington Quaker businessmen, Edward Pease of the Pease family's wool mill and Jonathan Backhouse of the Backhouse Bank, financed the railway's construction. When I realized that the locomotive that had hauled the first train was the one I had seen on the platform of Darlington's Bank Top main line station on the first day I arrived in the town, it became clear that I had truly come to my 'spiritual home'.

As my knowledge of early railway history increased I realized that North Road station was at the very heart of that great heritage. The very first passenger train had stopped at the North Road site on the historic day of 27 September 1825. As though by some turn of fate, my first summer holiday from school

Locomotion No. 1 *in 1975 when it was still sited at Bank Top Main Line Station. (Copyright,* The Northern Echo)

George Stephenson's Locomotion *on display in North Road railway museum.* (*Copyright, Ray Allison*)

began from North Road station and I could enter its fascinating interior with all the privileges of a fare-paying passenger.

The station was a complete surprise, but a most pleasant one to a new visitor. Approaching the station was rather like arriving at a country house. Its graceful windows, stylish chimney stacks and rendered walls rather than smoke-blackened brick raised holiday spirits to a high level. The inside of the station offered every comfort to awaiting passengers. There was a simple island platform reached by a footbridge. Trains for the west came in at one side and trains returning to Darlington at the other.

As a comparative newcomer to the Northeast I was fascinated by the destinations I saw on the boards, many of which were on the other side of England. Tebay and Kirby Stephen were in a county called Westmoreland that would eventually disappear, except from the pages of history. There was Penrith in the Lake District and a spur to Middleton-in-Teesdale. To complete the exciting list of destinations reached from the North Road station there was the Wearhead branch to Upper Weardale.

My parents were fortunate enough to have the use of a holiday cottage at Mickleton, the last railway station before the terminus at Middleton-in-Teesdale. I eagerly awaited the arrival of the Teesdale train and left the adults to select newspapers or magazines from the E.D. Walker and

Wilson newsagent's kiosk. These magazines have long passed into the history of British publishing, along with their quaint names. In the late thirties *Picture Post*, *Everybody's Tit-Bits* and *Lilliput* were popular reading in the comfortable passenger waiting room. The railway company whose trains ran through North Road station was the London and North Eastern Railway Company popularly known as the LNER. It must be admitted, however, that the Stockton and Darlington Railway in 1825 had given little consideration to the comfort of its passengers.

When the first train made its historic run in 1825 no station had been built at Darlington. A stop was made at Hopetown, a tiny village slightly northwest of Darlington and on the site of North Road station. A station for Darlington was not built until 1827 and its location was slightly to the east of the present site. Situated on the other side of North Road, or Durham Turnpike, the station was then in the countryside to the north of Darlington. If we take a £5 note from our wallet and look at George Stephenson's picture on the reverse side, the first Darlington railway station was just to the left of the famous Skerne Bridge pictured on the banknote.

The new station was a tall, rather utilitarian structure built against an embankment and set on a very small site. Passengers were faced with many flights of steps to reach platform level. The 'Stockton and Darlington' was certainly a public railway but it had been planned to carry coal from Shildon to the port of Stockton. Nevertheless, passengers were carried on the first run and were adventurous enough to share their accommodation with wagonloads of coal and flour! Company board members and town dignitaries fared rather better, travelling in a carriage modelled on the horse-drawn stagecoach,

A ride in the guard's van at North Road Railway Museum. (Copyright, Ray Allison)

Stockton and Darlington Railway Celebrations, August 1975. Revd Eric Treacy speaking at Darlington's Bank Top Station. (Copyright, The Northern Echo)

which the railway would eventually replace.

As the new railway system expanded, the station at Skerne Bridge became inadequate. There was no space for sidings or an engine shed. A new station was planned on the other side of the turnpike highway, which in present day Darlington is High Northgate. The new station was opened in 1842 with a large site providing space for sidings and an engine shed.

The original building was a long single-storey façade featuring windows in the Georgian style, though Queen Victoria was by then the reigning monarch. In 1873 an upper storey was added, still featuring Georgian windows and a shallow pitched roof, echoing the Regency style of architecture. It became a building displaying a classical elegance which fortunately still remains today. The old lane named Whessoe Lane was planned to lead directly to the station and was renamed Station Road. By this time railway passengers had been recognized as an important source of revenue and the new station was planned to cater for their every comfort.

The Decades of Destiny

A centenary for such an historic station would in normal circumstances be cause for great celebration, but in 1942 North Road and indeed the entire railway network of

Britain was battling to survive the Second World War. The station was surrounded by heavy industry such as Whessoe, the North Road locomotive works and Rise Carr steel rolling mills, all working day and night for the war effort.

Thankfully, North Road survived intact, but I do recall one bomb which must have been classified as a 'near-miss'. It landed one evening when I was visiting the home of friends in Wilson Street with my parents. A mighty explosion announced a flying visit by the *Luftwaffe* to Darlington. It brought down flakes of plaster from the ceiling and rattled the best china on the dining room table, but fortunately missed the packed terraced streets of Hopetown. It missed North Road station and according to my father, the Whessoe works. Popular opinion had it falling between the latter and the railway offices at Stooperdale on Brinkburn Road. If it landed on allotments in that area it could have done no more than make a slight dent in Britain's 'Dig for victory' campaign!

The railway survived the war, but in 1948 faced a further challenge when the entire British network was nationalized. The four private companies, which had served the entire United Kingdom, were amalgamated into one giant company and given the title, 'British Railways'. By the 1950s the new network was facing serious financial problems and a certain Dr Beeching was appointed to prepare a report and recommend a viable solution. In the simplest terms his report suggested that all lines failing to show a profit should be closed. These Draconian measures were accepted and railway routes all over Britain were closed by a process infamously known as 'The Beeching Axe'. Branch railways suffered most heavily and as almost all of Darlington's railway connections to the west were threatened, North Road's future was placed in grave doubt. These links survived the 1950s, but in the following decade 'The Beeching Axe' was wielded to deadly effect.

The trans-Pennine link was closed, its track lifted and great viaducts dismantled. The Middleton-in-Teesdale spur was also closed and the upper Weardale branch from Bishop Auckland retained only as a freight line. Fortunately, the Darlington to Bishop Auckland route stayed on as a passenger line saving the eight miles of 'heritage railway' between North Road station and Shildon. North Road thus survived as a passenger station.

North Road steams back

Though North Road had escaped what amounted to a death threat, in the 1960s its sidings became a gloomy graveyard for steam locomotives facing dismantling and consignment to the scrap yard. I was saddened to see the sturdy A8 tank engines, which had served the Pennine link so faithfully, crumble under the oxyacetylene torch. As diesel powered propulsion replaced 135 years of steam, *Evening Star* was the last steam locomotive to be built for regular railway service. Steam power had reached the end of the line, yet by a strange turn of fate North Road would have the last word on the subject.

In 1975 celebrations planned for the 150th anniversary of the Stockton and Darlington Railway proved to be North Road Station's salvation. The showpiece event was a great 'steam-past' of classic steam locomotives from the nineteenth and twentieth centuries. This was held at Shildon near the start of the first railway. I was fortunate enough to attend this highly successful event, which attracted visitors from all over the world. As a permanent commemoration, railway museums would be established at Shildon and North Road Station. The latter would still serve as a passenger station on the Darlington to Bishop Auckland line with an entrance from McNay Street off High Northgate. Shildon would adapt the cottage home of Timothy Hackworth, George Stephenson's maintenance engineer, at the nearby Shildon locomotive works to form part of the museum.

The Duke of Edinburgh opened North Road Railway Museum on 27 September 1975. Pride of place in the 'locomotive hall' created by filling in the open ends of the station went to *Locomotion*, George Stephenson's No. 1 engine that he had driven on the historic first run. Until 1975 *Locomotion* stood proudly with *Derwent*, another early steam locomotive at Darlington's Bank Top Station on the main line. Also acquired for the museum was John Dobbin's classic painting, *Opening of the Stockton and Darlington railway*. *Derwent* and *Locomotion* came to North Road as part of a high quality collection of steam locomotives representing the nineteenth and twentieth centuries. Inside, rooms adjoining the locomotive hall feature priceless artefacts relating to the early operation of railways.

The new museum was well established when in the late 1990s an exciting project was started at the Hopetown carriage works adjoining the station's former sidings. The 'Tornado project' involved the construction of a new steam locomotive that would be fully operational on all parts of the railway system. The locomotive would be the first to be built in Britain for over forty years and its design would be a revival of the A1 Pacific class *Peppercorn*, a powerful locomotive which had hauled express trains on the East

Coast main line. The project would revive Darlington's traditional locomotive industry that had ended with the closure of the North Road locomotive works in the 1950s. More steam locomotives would be built at Hopetown creating a second era for Darlington's traditional industry.

North Road railway museum is now a living heritage that attracts visitors of all ages and backgrounds. At its bank holiday events and during Darlington's September railway carnival children can enjoy activities on a spacious green created at the site of former railway sidings. From here they can board a goods train and ride in the guard's van alongside the Hopetown carriage works where the Tornado steam locomotive is being built. When the museum hosts model collector's fairs I am delighted to join fellow 'Hornby boys' who eagerly seek out the tinplate treasures of the famous Hornby model trains.

The trains of North Road are now still and silent, their gleaming livery reflecting glory gone, but not forgotten. Those of us who recall happy days of steam travel will appreciate the museum's preservation of our memories in such pristine perfection. With world railway heritage site status awaiting confirmation, generations who have admired North Road as both station and museum will look to the future and offer grateful thanks for its glorious past.

Ray Allison

The Grand Steam Cavalcade

Sunday 31 August 1975 and the Grand Steam Cavalcade was coming to Darlington to celebrate 150 years of the Darlington to Stockton Railway. Approximately thirty of the finest steam engines ever made were to travel between Shildon and Darlington.

I was seven years old and had never seen a working steam train. My Dad, on the other hand, had seen many. I remember he had looked forward to the event for months and when the day arrived he could hardly contain his excitement.

We lived on Haughton Road in front of Jollys Timber Yard and right next to the main east coast line. From our back garden you could see every train that went past.

The day of the cavalcade was warm and sunny, perfect weather my Dad had said. The engines were leaving Shildon at two o'clock and I remember watching from our garden as people arrived early to get a good viewpoint. The bridge over the railway line was crowded by one o'clock and people jostled with each other to see. The land at the side of our house was also quickly filling, although it actually belonged to the railways and technically spectators were trespassing, but nobody seemed to care, everyone just wanted to see the steam engines.

My Dad kept checking the time and lots of friends and family were arriving to watch from our garden. Some of us kids had to stand on boxes and chairs in order to see over the fence. My Mam provided a constant flow of refreshments; tea, coffee, pop, beer and home made ice-lollies.

Eventually, after what seemed like hours of waiting, the first signs of the cavalcade appeared. Puffs and puffs of white smoke billowed across the sky like balls of fluffy cotton wool, then the gleaming green paint of the first engine passed by. Magnificent!

My Dad decided he wanted an even closer look and ordered everyone out of the garden and onto the railway land at the side. We all followed and sat as close to the track as possible.

Engine after engine passed by in an array of colours; red, blue, green and burgundy, all gleaming brightly. The gold lettering of their names and numbers sparkled as the afternoon sun caught each one. The Leander, Sir Nigel Gresley and Mallard among them.

I had never seen or heard or smelled anything like it. The engines were huge, the noise of the pistons hypnotic and the smell of the smoke addictive. My Dad was childlike as he cheered and waved along with the rest of the huge crowd that had lined the bridge and track.

The highlight of the day was seeing the *Flying Scotsman*. My Dad had talked about it over and over and now it was passing by right in front of us. At the front were two small wheels under the black funnel, which stood aloft the curved front panel. Then there were three huge wheels, which carried the blue engine, number 4498. The driver was waving proudly from his cab and everyone waved and cheered and clapped as he tooted his whistle as he passed by.

My Dad couldn't stop smiling, even after the last engine had passed by and all the smoke had cleared from the sky. I had never understood why he had been so fascinated by steam engines, but after 'The Grand Steam Cavalcade' I wondered no more.

Janet Heath

Wartime At Stivvies

Jack was an apprentice draughtsman at Robert Stephenson Locomotive Works, Darlington in 1941. Being nineteen years of age and having done three years in the drawing office, he was transferred to do his year of practical work in the factory, before returning to the drawing office to complete his apprenticeship.

After two months in the machine shop turning axle cover plates for military tank axles, he was moved to the erecting shop, to more interesting and exciting work. He would be erecting and dismantling a locomotive, and not just any locomotive. It was the last of four for the Iraqi railways, which was urgently required for wartime duty. They were steam engines, fuelled by oil, of which Iraq had plenty! They were to be designed, built, tested, dismantled, packed and then taken by road for shipment to Iraq.

It was hard work in hard times. There were long hours of work along with cycling to work up and down the old A1, now North Road in Darlington. This was a total daily distance of more than 10 miles. Working days included early morning starts, long hours of work, overtime, and then night classes (if you had not obtained a higher national certificate in mechanical engineering by the age of twenty-one, you would be sacked). Fire watching and the home guard took more spare time, as it was the time of rationing and the blackout.

There was football, however. The firm's junior team, the Rocket Juniors had reached the final of the Darlington Junior League Cup. The Rocket playing field was adjacent to the works and in it was the clubhouse and canteen. The committee of the club were all male and elderly and only they had keys. None of them wanted to have to open up on Saturday afternoons to get the goal netting, flagpoles and balls out before a match. They solved the problem by making Jack a committee member who would than have a key and also the right to attend meetings. At one meeting a letter was read out complaining that some of the team members had been using strong language. The chairman finished the letter and said, 'We must do something to stop these young buggers from using this bloody awful language.' To Jack's amazement not one of the committee members could see anything incongruous in what he said! They all knew him. It was the way he talked. It was the way they talked. Was it any wonder that the youths were beginning to talk that way!

The League Cup Final would be Jack's best game ever, but he would need the time off work to play. The foreman was a tall thin man who walked very fast. Almost running to keep up with him, Jack told him they were in the final, and asked whether he could have the day off. 'No you flipping can't!' he was told as the foreman walked away. Jack is not sure that flipping was the word he used, but is sure that it began with an F. He was devastated, gutted, and sick as a parrot, to use today's figures of speech. But that was it!

Back at work, Jack still remembers the hard physical graft of being given an enormous file with which to clean the cowcatcher after it had been forged and burnt out. It was his first job on the engine and they were testing him. How would he cope?

He also remembers nearly losing an index finger. They were removing the dome from its flange on the top of the boiler. Jack was perched up on high removing the nuts to allow the dome to be lifted off by the 50 ton capacity overhead crane. He had slackened them all by spanner and was screwing the last part of the threads by hand. As he was on the last nut, the crane driver mistook a signal from below and lifted. His finger was being trapped. He yanked it out just in time but it was a mess, badly torn and blood everywhere. The scar is still there today.

Another memory is of one of the foremen who would break up a group of lads who were talking instead of working with the biblical words, 'Wheresoever two or three of ye shall be gathered together, there shall I be amongst you.'

The toilet facilities were Victorian, communal, side-by-side and back-to-back. The custodian's unofficial but universal job description was 'shithouse clerk'. Jack maintained that the main qualification must have been a sense of smell very well below the average.

As you entered the toilet you gave him your works number. You had five minutes and if you weren't out by then he would report you and you would lose an hour's pay. The custodians name was Davy Jones. Amongst the general graffiti conspicuously placed, was a poem that read; 'Do not come here to sleep or slumber, for Davy Jones has got your number!' Everyone had heard of the day that a prankster, who from the top of the flush channel, had set fire to a piece of paper, then floated it downstream under the bums of the occupants.

Now back to our locomotive. One of the foremen went to Iraq to supervise the erection and re-testing of the locos. Jack's loco was on its way to Iraq, round South Africa and into the Red Sea, when the ship and its contents were sunk by enemy action. For Jack that news was even worse than not playing in the final.

All that work on the lovely locomotive! It had involved designers, manufacture of parts by platers, and forgemen, boilermakers, pattern makers, coppersmiths and many more. But then the loco was a very small part of the ship's cargo. It had all gone. The ship itself had gone.

Dozens of other ships were going, like this, all the time. What a lesson to Jack, and to us all, of the madness of war.

In the war, cost did not matter. The millions of men in the services were paid, the workers were paid, and money was no object. Yet now, sixty years on, we seem to find it so difficult to replace a school or hospital, and to run the railways.

John Smith

The Neasham Road Trolley

Younger readers may think that this is a tale about a local supermarket, but it is, in fact, a tale about the Darlington trolleybus, which disappeared from the streets in 1957. Most Darlingtonians aged over fifty will remember these strange contraptions which provided public transport in the town for over thirty years.

Darlington is not my native town and, as I came to the town to live in the mid-1970s, I have no first-hand knowledge of these vehicles. I was born in a West Yorkshire town that had an extensive trolleybus system operated by large double deckers, all six-wheelers and able to swallow up crowds of seventy or more at a time. One of my best friends at grammar school had family connections with Darlington (his mother, maiden name Dorothy Henderson came from here) and he told me of his trips to the North East. Being interested in trolleybuses, I was anxious to know about those in Darlington and one day he produced some photographs and I could hardly believe my eyes! Here was pictured no sleek modern double decker that I was used to, but a very small single decker, a virtual biscuit tin on wheels with two very long, trolley poles reaching up to the power lines above. The bus had just passed under a railway bridge

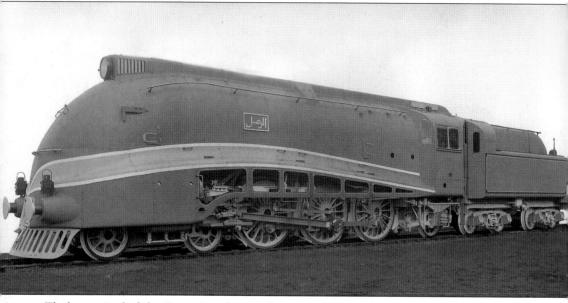

The locomotive built by 'Stivvies', Robert Stephenson and Co. Ltd for use by Iraqi Railways, 1941.

and was turning right at a road junction. The single destination sign read 'Neasham Road'.

This was my first startling introduction to the Darlington trolleybus and from then on I was interested in finding out more. Little did I know at the time that I would in later life obtain a position with Darlington's Corporation Transport Department and remain with them planning timetables and scheduling buses and staff through privatisation in the 1980s right to the rather bitter end of the council owned bus service in 1994; and that my home in Darlington would be, and still is, situated on Neasham Road!

Trolleybuses came to the town in 1926 and replaced the trams as well as opening up entirely new routes such as the short run along Neasham Road which never had trams. Because of restrictions caused by the many low railway bridges in the town, which at that time crossed most of the main

roads, the trolleybuses had to be single deckers. Although they used the same electricity as the trams, they did not need rails and ran on rubber tyres with the power coming from the overhead cables which mapped out the trolleybus routes 16ft above the road.

Where routes diverged, the trolley poles on the bus had to be diverted onto the required path. This was done manually by the conductor running from the bus and holding down a lever at a roadside pole as the trolleys passed over the points. Eventually, at the busiest junctions such as Bank Top/Neasham Road and North Road/Station Road, electric devices were inserted into the overhead wires allowing the driver to select the desired route by applying power as the trolley arms passed over a skate. In the Market Place/High Row area, lay-by loops were inserted into the overhead wires to allow one trolleybus to overtake another. The only other way of overtaking was for the driver of the front vehicle to lower the trolley arms to allow the one behind to pass. On occasions at junctions or through excessive speed on curves, the trolley arms would leave the wires, bringing the bus to an involuntary halt and leaving the poles swinging helplessly in the air. They had to be retrieved by the crew using a bamboo pole with a hook on the end which was kept under the bus for this purpose.

All the trolleybuses had central entrances, seated about thirty-two passengers and were painted dark blue, though this was changed later to a lighter shade. By the early part of the Second World War there were over sixty trolleybuses in operation, and many of the newer ones were of a modern streamlined shape. The transport system was regarded as an efficient compact unit serving the needs of the town and indeed Darlington was one of only two towns in the country whose corporation transport was run entirely with trolleybuses, (the other being Ipswich).

The routes operated were:

Trolleybus in Bondgate en route to Faverdale. The overhead wires branching off to the right allowed trolleybuses to do a U-turn in Bondgate to return to the Market Place. To make this manoeuvre the conductor would have to jump off the bus and pull a handle on the adjacent pole to divert the trolley arms onto the correct wires.

Trolleybus turning from Bondgate beside the Pease monument on its way to Neasham Road, around 1956. The road layout at this point has significantly changed.

1 – Eastbourne (Lingfield Lane) to Harrowgate Hill (Longfield Road End);

2 – Haughton (Barmpton Lane End) to Harrowgate Hill;

3 – Faverdale to Neasham Road (Geneva Road);

4 – Coniscliffe Road (Baydale Road) to Cockerton (Travellers Rest) via Station Road and Willow Road, returning via Woodland Road;

5 – Park Lane (Parkside) to Cockerton (Traveller's Rest) via Woodland Road, returning via Willow Road and Station Road.

A regular service operated at peak times on the Harrowgate Hill route as far as Brougham Street, where buses reversed into Cumberland Street to turn. The terminus at Park Lane also involved buses reversing.

By 1943 the original 1926 trolleybuses were worn out and government permission was granted to buy twenty-four new trolleybuses to replace them. Due to the national emergency these were of 'no frills' utility construction with wooden slatted seats and angular bodywork. Only thirty of these single deckers were ever built and all but six came to Darlington. The wooden seats were replaced by cushioned ones after the war except for the bench seat opposite

Trolleybus turning at the Neasham Road Terminus, c. 1956.

the entrance. These were the vehicles that ran to the end of the trolleybus era.

After the war, the tide began to turn against the trolleybus for various reasons. The electric power for the vehicles was generated at the corporation's own power station next to the depot in Haughton Road, but from 1948 power generation was nationalized, depriving the corporation of cheap electricity. There were also plans to divest the transport function of the corporation into a regional transport authority. Closer to home, new housing estates were springing up on the edges of the town at places such as Firth Moor and Springfield and to serve these by trolleybus would require substantial investment in new overhead equipment. One short extension to the system did open in 1949 when the Eastbourne service was lengthened from Lingfield Lane to McMullen Road to serve the factory at Patons & Baldwins. This was largely funded by Patons & Baldwins themselves.

Despite this uncertainty, and relying on the intention to lower the road under the railway bridges on the 'main line' Eastbourne to Harrowgate Hill service, six fifty-six-seater double-decker trolleybuses entered service in 1949 to cater for the heavy traffic on this service (it served North Road Railway repair shops). In the event they were restricted to the Park Lane to Cockerton service as the bridges remained stubbornly low and these fine buses were sold three years later for further service in Doncaster and eventually Bradford.

Despite this, the decision was made to introduce services into the new estates using diesel buses and then to gradually replace the trolleys with these over the next decade. The

Trolleybus in leafy Woodland Road, 1957. (Copyright Photobus, J. Copland)

process started in 1951 when the last trolleybus ran to Harrowgate Hill. By 1954, when the Coniscliffe Road to Cockerton service went over to diesel buses, there was just one main route left, between Faverdale and Neasham Road, with a peak hour service also running between Brougham Street and McMullen Road. This latter service saw its last trolleybus in 1956 leaving just one route left run by eight of the wartime 'biscuit tin' trolleybuses.

Many of the redundant trolleybuses were sold to Bradford Corporation where they were eventually rebuilt out of all recognition with very modern front entrance double-decker bodywork and as such ran in the Yorkshire city until the early 1970s. The only clue that they once ran in Darlington was the GHN Darlington registration letters on the number

plate.

One of these buses ran in Bradford during 1957 in its single-decker Darlington form (where it was known as 'the pup'), due to the Suez crisis which imposed fuel restrictions. The opportunity was taken to run this bus instead of a diesel bus thereby saving fuel. Back in Darlington, The Suez crisis was also prolonging the lives of the remaining trolleys and they soldiered on in Woodland Road and Neasham Road until permission was granted by the Ministry of Transport for more diesel buses to be run. The end came on Wednesday 31 July 1957 when the trolleys ran a normal service and that was that. Next day the new buses took over and a few days later they were extended beyond the roundabout at Geneva Road into Brankin Road.

The local press (*Northern Despatch*) did mention the event with the heading 'End of an Era' and went on – 'Quietly and unobtrusively the last of Darlington's trolleybuses has been taken off the roads and the changeover to motorbuses is now complete. No more will we see trolley arms weaving wildly in the air and sweating conductors wrestling with unwieldy poles in an attempt to get them back in place. Although some people agree that the (diesel) buses are better in a town like Darlington, there are those who regret seeing the last of the 'trolleys' and it would have been nice, I think to have had some ceremony last Wednesday when the last trolleybus ran for the last time.'

Yes it would. In my West Yorkshire town the last trolleybus was an occasion when the mayor and corporation turned out; the last bus was festooned in coloured lights like a Blackpool tram and literally hundreds turned out to watch it pass.

A shame for the little biscuit tin trolleybus on Neasham Road.

Steve Lockwood

Trolleybus entering the town centre at Stonebridge on a journey from Neasham Road. Note the electricity power station cooling towers in the background still showing wartime camouflage paint. 1957. (Copyright Photobus, J. Copland)

Patons & Baldwins, 1963. (Copyright, The Northern Echo)

Training instructress at work Patons & Baldwins, 1968. (Copyright, The Northern Echo)

Patons & Baldwins Textile Factory, 1961 (Copyright, The Northern Echo)

CHAPTER 5
Sport and Pastimes

Darlington Railway Institute who were playing against Northallerton College in the North Riding Senior Cup, Northallerton College, 1961.

Early Cycling In South Durham

The first cycling club to be formed in the four Northern counties was Darlington Bicycle Club, in 1876. R.B. Summerson, had ridden a 'boneshaker' as a youngster.

Boneshakers were simple machines made during the 1860s of iron, and had a front wheel with steering-head and pedals.

The boneshaker soon gave way to the era of the high-wheeler or 'ordinary' bicycle firmly established by the late 1870s. These 'penny-farthings' were driven on the boneshaker principle of cranks and pedals attached to the front wheel, that, in order to achieve optimum gearing, increased in size over the years.

By 1878, South Durham boasted seven bicycle clubs. Organized cycling north of the Tees was given added impetus by the staging of the North East 'meets'. Little is known of the 1876 and 1877 excursions; the 1878 gathering at Morpeth thereafter called the First Annual Meet. Stockton Amateur Bicycle Club is believed to have been represented, as, quite probably, was Darlington BC. Darlington was the venue of the Harrowgate Meet, known to have been held from 1876 to at least 1879.

Stockton Amateur BC had been formed in 1878, based on the town's YMCA. Once constituted, the running of a club revolved around the key posts of secretary and treasurer. Apart from the usual committee members, there would be a captain, with a deputy, lieutenant, and one or more buglers. On the weekly club run, generally held on a Saturday afternoon and soon to become a venerated institution of the pastime, the captain came into his own. Aided by his subordinate officers, he maintained strict two-by-two formation.

The elaborate uniform of Stockton Amateur BC included an engraved belt, and was topped by a turban or straw hat depending on the season. The club arranged their first ever club run to take in Mount Grace Priory, Stokesley and Great Ayton on Easter Monday, 1878. The secretary inspected the route beforehand and reported on the state of the roads. Good Friday saw a trial run by the club to High Leven; on Saturday a 'drill run' to Sadberge took place. Also in 1878, the newly formed Stockton Bicycle Club set out for Northallerton on their first club run. *The Middlesbrough News* reported, 'A large number of the inhabitants turned out to see their departure.'

The novelty of the bicycle meant that cycling was very much in the public eye. The local press gave over thirty lines to an incident in 1879 concerning a Teesside 'bicyclist' in collision with a cow. Darlington Bicycle Club members appeared at Stockton County Court early in 1878 charged with riding on the footpath. (They often provided a superior surface to roads). The cyclists lost the case, but the following year, Fred Dodds, a Cambridge University BC member, successfully prosecuted a farmer who blocked the road with his horse and cart, and, as reported in *Bicycling* (1879), 'in a highly offensive manner informed Mr Dodds that he had no right on the road with such a machine.' The chairman of the Stockton Bench concurred and, 'regretted the law was not on the defendant's side, as bicycles were thorough nuisances on highways.' Had Dodds' father not been an MP, it is doubtful that he would have won.

Many were the problems facing early cyclists. They were often ridiculed or vilified, even physically attacked, whether by stone-throwing urchins, or coachmen recognizing the threat from this faster mode of travel that upset horses.

Gradually though, the cyclist became less and less *persona non grata*. Commercial interests were well served by an increasing demand for cycles. Innkeepers found that the new breed of traveller ate and drank heartily.

By 1880 the bicycle was well on the way to becoming part of popular culture. This can be gauged by an advertisement in *The Daily Gazette* during April of that year. Stockton Skating Rink played host to 'Srik's

Troup of Male and Female Bicycle Equestrians' including 'wondrous little Baby Bicyclist Florrie, only four years of age.'

Part of the programme at the rink was a one-mile bicycle race. At first, cycling events were novelties on the programme of 'Sports' meetings, the cyclist taking second place to runners, and using athletes' tracks of grass or cinders, Darlington Cricket and Football Club Sports of 1876 being an early example. September 1880 witnessed the arrival of Waller's portable wooden track and marquee. Separate races were held for amateurs and professionals, the latter competing for £50 and a gold medal over six days, 5,000 attending the final night. 'Waller's Pavilion' toured the North East, stopping at Middlesbrough, Stockton, Darlington and Bishop Auckland.

Tricycles were rarely raced because they existed primarily as a sedate alternative to the high-wheeler for the short, the less athletic, the not so young, and women. An expensive piece of machinery that climbed only with difficulty, the three-wheeler seems to have been more popular in the South. Their heyday was around 1883. The Stanley Show at The Albert Hall that year exhibited 233 bicycles, 289 tricycles.

Only one, short-lived, club solely for tricycles appears to have existed in South Durham. Twelve members of 'Stockton TC' applied for Cyclists' Touring Club membership during 1884. (The national CTC had changed its name from Bicycle Touring Club in order to accommodate tricyclists.) The dozen named include five merchants, a doctor, and a solicitor and his wife. Tricycling was clearly a middle-class activity.

Given the immanent social divisions of Victorian England, cycling could hardly be immune to class distinctions. In one area of cycling, sport, the working man had already made a significant impact. This exacerbated the conflict of professionalism and amateurism. Amateurs could be banned from racing and expelled from their club if found 'guilty' of racing against professionals. Presumably the Wharton brothers transgressed this rule, for, although members of Darlington Bicycle Club and slate merchants, they were declared 'professionals' in 1855.

Closely allied to the argument of professionalism is the matter of betting. Charles Ashurst resigned at the end of 1893 as Secretary of Hartlepool's Social and Cycling Club in protest at 'bookmakers' and 'professional gamblers' being admitted to the membership.

Another shibboleth of the age, Temperance, affected the pastime. This was hardly surprising as cycling is an activity liable to create a thirst, and alternatives to alcoholic beverages and public houses were slow to develop. By 1893 Darlington had a (albeit short-lived) Temperance Cycling Club. That year the *Darlington Temperance Chronicle* criticized the shop workers' Darlington Wednesday CC for allowing themselves to be photographed in front of a public house (probably club headquarters). Pubs were generally an integral part of club life. Reporting on a Stockton Rovers run to Hartlepool in 1892, the Cycling Correspondent of the *Northern Review* asked, 'Who was that cyclist seen with a life-buoy round his neck crawling along the promenade?' The *North-Eastern Daily Gazette* recorded that in 1893 Alderman Thomas Wrightson MP, in opening new clubrooms for the Old Castle CC in Stockton, commented that previously most meetings were at pubs, but a cyclist needs to 'preserve himself from pernicious habits.'

Gladstone Street School cricket team, 1950-51.

West Hartlepool's Grosvenor CC also opened new club premises. The *North-Eastern Daily Gazette* reported that Capt. W. Tomlinson, Club President, 'had undertaken to pay the rent of the club for one year on condition that intoxicating liquors were not introduced.'

Another contentious issue was Sunday cycling. The Cyclists' Touring Club advised its members to hide the Club's badge before sallying forth a wheel on the Sabbath. Official all-day Sunday club rides were rare before 1900.

Important technological developments were changing the world of cycling during the second half of the 1880s. The rear wheel chain-driven bicycle began to be produced in quantity from 1885. Known as the 'Safety', this design, akin to that of the modern bicycle, gradually superseded the 'ordinary' and diminished the importance of the tricycle.

Consequently ladies increasingly took to two wheels. Women accounted for around one quarter of local applications for CTC membership during the late 1890s. Most were middle-class and often related to CTC members. Women were not encouraged to race. The *North-Eastern Daily Gazette* noted that the National Cyclists' Union in 1895, 'moved that the permit for the Hartlepool Social CC (*sic*) sports be withdrawn if the ladies' race would tend to lower it, and to reduce the number of lady cyclists.'

Cycling appeared everywhere, from Christmas pantomime at Stockton to the 'World Champion Trick Cyclist' at Bishop Auckland. At West Hartlepool, over ten miles, two cyclists raced on public roads for a £10 wager, the winner being one-legged. The vice-captain of Richmond CC raced the Darlington train (and only lost by ten minutes).

The Marquis of Londonderry organized the Londonderry Benevolent CC. This consisted of two sections, each based on his estates: Wynard Park and Seaham. Although patronage met some incidental expenses of ordinary members (including, surprisingly, alcoholic beverages) the club does not seem to have enjoyed much popularity. Perhaps a club that promised, 'stability and discipline' lacked appeal.

'Respectable' clubs of a religious, political or Temperance persuasion, like those run on paternalistic lines, never proved popular in the region. Works' teams existed, briefly; presumably people did not wish to be reminded of their jobs during leisure hours. Hence Teesside CC of Stockton, consisting mostly of employees of the shipbuilders Craig & Taylor, could not claim many members.

One reason such clubs failed to recruit many of the wheeled fraternity is that they tended to neglect the sporting sphere and were inclined to shy away from National Cyclists' Union affiliation. During the 1891 off-season Middlesbrough Amalgamated Cycling Clubs called a meeting with the intention of setting up a local centre of the NCU. As three clubs apiece from Stockton and Hartlepool sent representatives to this initial meeting, NCU Headquarters was asked to include South Durham in the centre.

The most important and lasting development arising from the North York (sic) and South Durham Local Centre was its adoption of the Richmond Whitsun Meet. Since 1886 the region's enthusiasts had congregated at Barnard Castle at Whitsuntide. Despite the location being nearer to Teesside than Tyneside, Northumberland and North Durham continued to dominate the proceedings, both on the organizing committee and in the number of participants. The 1886 Barnard Castle programme shows the probable number of visiting North Riding and South Durham Club members to be about fifty; that for Northumberland and North Durham to be nigh on two hundred. Richmond Meet attracted all walks of life: the 1894 edition's opening parade contained twenty-one riders belonging to Stokesley CC; the same number came according to the *Northern Review*, 'in their pit costume' from Wingate, a County Durham colliery village, under the banner of Station Town Brothers CC.

Three of the top local racing men of the 1890s were coal miners. Tommy Childs, the most prolific winner of this Ferryhill trio, won the prestigious Manchester Wheelers' Muratti Cup. Childs and his two colleagues, Davies and Flatman, stayed loyal to Ferryhill CC, but at the same time, between them, belonged to seven other clubs. Changing clubs regularly suggests that some remuneration may have been involved. Miners' love of gambling is shown by the declarations recorded in the *North-Eastern Gazette* in 1897 of Davies challenging, 'any pitman in the world' to a race; and Childs' father 'to ride any man sixty years of age who has worked in the pits for forty years.'

Station Town riders parading in 'pit costume' shows that club uniforms were no longer popular, thus Darlington Tramps (copying Stockton Tramps, and Bohemians of Middlesbrough) insisted on no semblance of uniforms. During the

1890s cycling clubs of every description were in existence, from Auckland Ironworks CC to the 'Z' CC of Darlington. Everyone was catered for, from Stockton teachers to Darlington shop workers. Darlington offered cyclists the choice of at least eight clubs in 1891. Railway workers would have opted for Darlington North-Eastern, meeting at the Railway Tavern. Professional people and businessmen preferred the town's traditional Bicycle Club. Even Friendly Societies ran clubs for cyclists, for example, Darlington Help One Another CC. Politics also entered the cycling arena with Darlington Clarion (i.e. Socialist) and Hartlepool Liberals; the Conservatives had Coxhoe and District Primrose CC.

Club names often give a clue as to the membership. Stockton and Darlington again copied Middlesbrough with working-class 'Rovers', 'Victoria' and 'North End'. Grand titles such as Barnard Castle Excelsior Amateur CC suggest a 'superior' club. In 1891 The Excelsior suspended George Thompson for being a professional and asked J. Wright to resign for the same reason. Wright had been a committee member the previous year. Whether he was to resign from the committee or the club is unclear, but the reason was almost certainly because he became a partner in the region's most important cycle manufacturing firm, Wright, Shaw & Lingford. All three were Bishop Auckland Star members; Wright held the post of treasurer in 1893/94. The Star clearly did not bar those engaged in the cycle trade from holding office. During the same period their secretary was another Bishop Auckland cycle dealer and manufacturer.

Into a new century, and new clubs continued to emerge. Among them were Dolphin Khaki CC of Darlington who sported khaki caps, probably inspired by the Boer War; and Darlington St Augustine's for Catholics. Another new creation, Darlington Congregationalists' CC (the 'Three Cs') had a rule recorded in their Minute Book, 'Candidates for Membership must be over sixteen years of age and of good moral character.' This club refused to support the Darlington Cyclists' Charity Carnival suggesting that Church and Temperance cycling clubs review their attitude towards these functions, and see how they might be, 'supported in some way more in harmony with Christian principles.' If this appears to be rather uncharitable, the Congregational Church Secretary refused to allow a special board for Cycling Club notices.

Darlington BC, conscious of their early origins, tended to be conservative, and took until 1906 to introduce a Ladies' Section, albeit with a male secretary. Admitting women may have boosted numbers of both sexes. Darlington Wednesday became the largest club affiliated to the local centre and for many years numbered over 300 members.

As a pastime, the pleasures of cycling lessened in proportion to increases in motorised and horse-drawn traffic. The sport of cycling declined in popularity, with racing almost forced off the road, and the entrenchment of 'traditional' national games such as soccer and cricket. Depressed trade added to Durham's cycling problems. Doubts were even expressed, in 1913, over the continuing viability of that venerable institution – the Barnard Castle Meet. The First World War dealt the deathblow to many struggling clubs, and brought a dark end to a Golden Age of cycling.

Bob Goodall

A Darlington Bowling Legend

Who was the man who put Darlington on the map in the world of sport, nearly forty years ago? Well, his name was John Leslie Watson, known as Les, and he was my father. He was born in Darlington in 1909 and died 1 April 1991. He was born into an ordinary working class family, his father worked for the *Northern Echo*, and he had two brothers, Alan and Harry and a sister Renie. During his early years he played tennis, table tennis and football but it was in lawn bowls that he went onto achieve his fame.

He joined East Park Bowling club along with his brother Harry and sister Renie. He went on to win all their competitions

Harry and Les Watson with the English Bowling Association National Pairs Championship Trophy, 1956.

including champion of champions a number of times and both brothers and sister were picked to play for Durham at county level.

In 1956 Harry and Les, who had played together since 1948, went on to win the English Bowling Association National Pairs Championship and were nicknamed the 'Giant Killers'. They were two of the youngest players in the competition, Harry forty-three and Les forty-six. It was the first time ever that a National Trophy had been won for East Park. In 1967 Les reached the semi-finals in the same competition. This time he was playing with a friend and fellow East Park player Edgar Cossins.

In May 1958 Les was nominated and selected to play in the trial match to qualify to play for England but sadly was not selected at this time. In 1959 both brothers were nominated and Les was selected to play and Harry was chosen as reserve. In 1960 both were again in the trials and Les was selected a second time. Both were back in the trials again in 1961 and this time both were chosen to play for England. It was the first time that brothers had been picked for the same England team and also the first time that two County Durham players were selected. The England team went on to win for the seventh time in eight years.

Les was again chosen to play for England in 1962 and played with Sid Drysdale, Tom Fleming and David Bryant. These four formed the rink which 'scooped the green' by winning all of their matches in the tournament at Eastbourne. The year 1962 was very good for Les as he was also nominated and finally selected to play in the British Empire and Commonwealth Games held in Perth, Australia along with the other three players named above. These four went on to make a name for themselves in Australia and finally won a Gold Medal,

From left to right: Dave Bryant, Les Watson, Sid Drysdale and Tom Fleming pictured with their gold medals at the British Empire and Commonwealth Games in Perth, Australia, 1962.

the ultimate achievement for any sportsman. Les also reached the play-offs for the Bronze medal in the pairs competition. He was partnered with Tom Fleming but they were beaten into fourth place by Rhodesia.

Les achieved the ultimate accolade in 1963 by being nominated and selected not only to play for England but to also captain the England Team. This team went on to win the 1963 International Match.

Les then started to play indoor bowls first at Thornaby and then at The Morrison Centre, Darlington. He continued to enjoy the game of bowls until ill health prevented further participation.

E.J. Devine

Fishing Days

I bought a delicate split cane fly rod from Sweeney Todd's in Bucktons Yard a couple of years ago. I didn't really need it – I already had a perfectly good hollow glass fly rod. It was the label attached to it that hooked me.

It read, 'Originally sold by Cummins'. Now this may mean very little to anyone under thirty or to those who have never been interested in field sports but Cummins was an upmarket fishing tackle shop that used to be at the bottom of Coniscliffe Road. It was a shop that I remembered well from my schooldays. The building still looks the same today, from outside, with its Dickensian bow window but it's a beauty therapists now.

Forty years ago there would be an expensive display of fly rods, wicker creels, aluminium fly boxes and the like-tackle which my fishing friends and I had only seen as pictures in *Trout* and *Salmon* magazines in the dentist's waiting room.

Like most schoolboys who fished in those days we bought most of our fishing stuff – maggots, floats, hooks, ledgers etc. – at Elliot's in Duke Street or Wright's in Parkgate. Those were shops where we didn't feel out of place and where, come Sunday, the owners might well be pegged next to us in a fishing competition.

The few times I visited Cummins I always felt as though I should take my shoes off before I went in and it always seemed to me, probably unfairly, that hard-up schoolboys were not really wanted – the man behind the counter had bigger fish to fry.

It was not only that everything there seemed expensive or biased towards game fishing – from the glass topped counter with its myriad compartments of salmon and sea trout flies, and shining lures, to the breast waders and salmon rods. It was the 'Harrods' ambience which made me feel uncomfortable.

Not like at Elliot's or Wright's where they had practical equipment such as quills, bobs and pike-floats, maggot bags and keepnets, rod rests and haversacks. And out the back you knew there were barrels of sawdust heaving with maggots, a few chrysalises already forming on the top. Sixpence worth would be sufficient for a day's grayling fishing on the Tees or Swale.

But all three names, Cummin's, Elliot's and Wright's are just a memory now, as are so many places that played their part in our preoccupied world of fishing.

For example, further up Coniscliffe Road was R.J. Scott's, antiquarian booksellers, which I think was next to the North Bitchburn Fireclay Company Limited. It was in Scott's that I first saw a copy of *The Complete Angler* by Izaak Walton, although it was priced at a guinea and therefore far beyond my means as paperboy for Outhwaites, further up Coniscliffe Road, where I got my weekly copy of the *Angling Times*.

Back down and round the corner in Skinnergate was Wildsmiths shop, a name that, to older people in Darlington, evokes the smell of coffee beans roasting. It was there that we would take our Brooke Bond tea cards of freshwater fish to swap at the box in front of the counter. It is over twenty years since Wildsmiths closed in 1979.

Even with this exchange facility, almost no one seemed to be able to get the Perch card despite the unnecessary number of bags of tea our mothers were persuaded to buy. The only one of us with it in his collection had got it from a boy at another school in exchange for the middle page of his nude book which gives a pretty accurate idea of its rarity value.

Then towards the bottom of Duke Street was Knotts the general dealers where we bought enamel paint and balsa wood to make floats, and closer to home in Cleveland Terrace was Charltons the off licence that also sold bread and where we were given stale loaves to make groundbait.

None of these shops remain and yet there is still one place, relatively unchanged, which regularly reminds me of those 1960s fishing days.

About once a month I leave my car at the Victoria Road car park of the railway station en route to London. As I walk, pin-stripe suited, under the tunnel I am always reminded of forty years earlier when I would be hurrying for the 8.08 a.m. to Catterick Bridge. Then, instead of the polished brogues, the studs of my waders would scrape noisily on the stone floor and in place of my briefcase full of papers would be a canvas haversack crammed with tackle, flask and sandwiches. In my hand, which now carries a laptop, would be my fishing rod.

A short time later, as the 125 crosses the Tees at Croft Bridge, I can't help but think of those days when the old LNER train would have branched off to Moulton, Scorton and Catterick Bridge and I would have spent the day standing in the shallow rapids of the Swale rather than sitting in some claustrophobic high-rise city office.

I know which I prefer – and its not just nostalgia!

Alan Theakston

Feethams – 1984

Here I was at Darlington FC First Team training at fifteen years old. Talk about up there with the big boys.

Let's forget about the fact that Darlington in 1984 were (and in 2001 still are) a perennial lower division struggler. They had almost ceased to exist a couple of seasons previously. Exactly two years had elapsed

since Southampton manager Lawrie McMenemy brought a full-strength team including Kevin Keegan and World Cup winner Alan Ball to raise money to kick off the club's 'centenary celebrations'. In reality the gate receipts from the full-house earned a stay of execution from the Receiver, whilst an *Evening Despatch*-fronted fund ultimately saved, 'County Durham's last league club' from the very real threat of permanent extinction.

With an average home attendance of around 1,500 it beggars belief that they had come even this far. No, Darlington were never going to be a great team, and as a supporter you could not even pretend that they were a sleeping giant and dream of better things to come; a Utopian society with Darlington in the First Division slaying it out with Liverpool one week, Manchester United the next. It simply wouldn't have been right. Darlington were just destined to entertain the likes of Halifax, Bournemouth and Rochdale. Anyway, the biggest date in the Darlington calendar would always be versus Hartlepool and we would miss it too much. Unless, of course, 'Utopia' featured Hartlepool among the elite as well. We would rather remain in the Fourth Division. Darlington – a sleeping giant? More a dwarf with a hangover!

I had been to see my first game at Feethams as a ten-year-old at the back end of the 1978/79 season. It gets you. The pull that draws hundreds and thousands all over the country to their own gladiatorial duels every week. Though feelings of tribal belonging were well over my head, I did like the way the nets looked on the goal. Is that weird? I had never seen nets on goals before (being more intimately used to jumpers on the floor) and those fitted perfectly and were stretched taut into the ground. Silent

North Road Brass Shops football team around 1955-56.

sentinels of professionalism, a constant reminder that this was the real thing.

I soon cottoned on that Feethams was, uniquely, a football ground that enabled the fans to change ends at half time as well as the teams. A logistical nightmare in today's terms, the die-hards ambled away during the interval behind both the east and west stands, convening at the opposite end to ensure that they could 'welcome' the visiting goalkeeper en masse twice in one match – I often still wonder if visiting teams ever did a double-take upon reappearing for the second half, seeing identical faces behind the goal at both ends at the start of each half!

And so my early solo expeditions turned into a hard-core of half a dozen young teenagers. If we weren't ever-present home fans between 1982 and 1984, then I can't think why – there were no deaths or marriages in the immediate family. We simply loved Darlington FC. My Uncle Ken used to say, ' I bet they wouldn't come to see

you if you were bad.' I liked that. I always imagined goofy caricatures of them standing round a hospital bed holding flowers and fruit and trying to think of stuff to say.

Anyway, from the Tin Shed, naturally, we watched the men that were becoming our heroes – the actors of our fantasies. The young boy-done-good Fred Barber in goal, stalwarts Peter Skipper and Kevan Smith in defence, midfield iron from Dave McLean, midfield gloss from future Scotland International Dave Speedie, and forward class from Alan Walsh. Speedie kept the club in the national papers – it would not be long before Darlington did the Darlington thing and used him to pay off a few more debts. At least Walshy's goals kept us warm on the terrace for a good few years – he remains Darlington's all-time top scorer.

I coveted the green shirt, myself. I wanted to be a local boy-done-good, as well. And if, in a few years, Freddie was forced into some dream move to Liverpool because I had taken the number one shirt from him, well so be it. It's a funny old game, you know.

And now, during my 1984 Easter holidays, here I was in the ragged old Feethams East Stand changing rooms not 10ft from him. I can't remember how much sleep I'd had the night before; it can't have been much. For three months I'd been a trial-list goalkeeper with Darlington. Still in my final year at school, I attended training each Thursday night at the new Quaker Centre with the players that were the part-time members of the Darlington Reserves squad. I'd done ok, and one night Brian the coach asked me if I wanted to come along to First Team Training during my Easter holidays. Did I? Did I want to fulfil a dream by training with my teenage idols? You bet.

The familiar faces generally ignored me when I entered the dressing room but eyed me somewhat suspiciously when I started taking my clothes off, even though I had made a mental note to myself to look for names on pegs so I wouldn't pinch some old pro's place in the dressing room. No names, so I placed my bag next to a guy I didn't recognize who looked only a couple of years older than me. He was about the second youngest there, so I figured maybe we would have something in common. After a few polite words I discovered I was right. We

Gladstone Street School – Franklin House football team, 1950.

had loads in common – he was also a trial-list goalkeeper. Marvellous, I hadn't been told I had competition. He was about to be signed to Leicester City, so he said, but came up for the day out. I recognized this for the psychological gamesmanship it undoubtedly was. Was I involved with any other clubs? 'Oh…York,' I mumbled. If I was going to lie, I was going to make it as short as possible. The lightning bolt might have found me before I'd finished saying, 'Wolverhampton Wanderers.'

I pulled on my own green and black goalkeeper shirt and finally made eye contact with Fred Barber, who nodded his professional acknowledgement before returning to a conversation with Brian Honour about how many pints they had drunk the Saturday night before. 'Eight or nine' seemed to be the understandably vague agreement.

I deliberately didn't behave as absolutely completely awestruck as I felt. Sitting in the Feethams dressing room was as exhilarating an experience as I'd known. And yet overriding this was an enforced calmness. Have you ever realized you are standing in a queue next to someone famous? What do you do? Nine times out of ten, you ignore them. Maybe you ask for an autograph, I don't know. Either way, I can tell you that one thing you don't do when sitting half naked in the Feethams dressing room with your footballing idols, is tell them how much you adore them. I couldn't bring myself to mention the match I had watched them play the week before, and I couldn't even tell them that I was a regular on the terraces. Because you know what that would make me? It would make me a supporter. And I was here because I was trying to be a footballer. I was at this moment just some kid that had given the right name to the guy

on the front door before walking into the dressing room. Nothing more. I was clearly young, so maybe they would think I was some kind of goalkeeping prodigy to be invited in the first place. But they were professional footballers; they would make up their minds about me after they had seen me play. Ignore me before, perhaps accept me later. I could handle that; I had enough confidence in my abilities to let my abilities speak for themselves. So I ignored them right back because I wanted to be a professional footballer too.

We jogged up to the Abbey Road playing fields – the training ground at that time. Jogging always seems to be done in social-type clusters, which at least gave some the chance to find out my name and what I was doing here. I was pleased to make an early novelty-value impression. 'Fifteen? Here, Fred, watch yourself; this kid's only fifteen…' Ha! Darlington 1, Leicester City 0.

I can't remember much of the training session. I hear of footballers who played in a Cup Final saying the same thing. This was my cup final. I remember specialist goalkeeper fitness training, some running, lots of stretching, and not having much to do with the outfield players, except when I was one of three keepers chosen to take turns during shooting practice. I watched the first couple whiz past into the top corner at a million miles a second. I just stood, rooted. Maybe I was just a kid who had only played school football up until then. Perhaps I was overawed by my heroes stepping up to shoot at me? Actually, neither of these were factors. Far from it! In fact, I simply could not believe they could shoot that well! This prospective professional footballer's incapacitating observation had been, 'Why the bloody hell don't you do it like that on Saturday?' I

Darlington Railway Brass Shops football team probably 1956-57, during the Railway Association Medals Competition at the Railway Association Ground, Brinkburn Road.

quickly gathered myself together, raised my game to match theirs and started to pull out some great saves. I loved shot-stopping and I was good at it. I received some good encouragement from both Cyril and Fred at various times and thoroughly enjoyed myself. Yes it does beat working for a living.

Afterwards, back at Feethams in the East Stand changing rooms, I answered a few more questions about myself. 'Fifteen, yeah.' 'Hurworth School.' 'Easter Holidays.' It satisfied some and was a source of amusement to others. If I was a curiosity, then I'd accept that. It was better than anonymity and they were certainly giving me more eye contact than they had last time we were in here. It suddenly occurred to me that I hadn't disgraced myself and surely that's all I could have asked for.

After scrubbing up, I saw no reason to hang around. I politely said, 'Goodbye,' and 'See you around,' to those that met my eye as I left. Some of them said, 'See you later.' Could I read anything into that? No, I'd been very mature about the whole day so far and I wasn't going to start behaving like a fifteen-year-old.

I walked outside, feeling like I should go home and cross a couple of things off my List of Things To Do. Just think, even if I never made it as a professional, I'd somehow wangled my way into a professional club for a First Team Training session. But wait a second. Wangled? Strange, I couldn't shake the feeling. Maybe it was cold turkey after the high of the day so far. I'd lived a dream, and yet I was still just a school kid. I would be back to school in less than a fortnight. I had exams in two months' time. Even worse, my name wouldn't be one that Cyril Knowles would be considering for the coming League game. It suddenly occurred to me that I hadn't actually been formally introduced to the man himself. Other coaches had dealt with me throughout. As far as I knew, Cyril Knowles didn't, at any time, know who I was. Some kid that turned up maybe? 'Lets humour him and stick him in goal.'

I wasn't bad actually but nor was I at any time during that training session, really part of 'The Team'. With this, I realized that my true dream, therefore, remained unfulfilled. I'd trained and been goalkeeper for a couple of hours, but that didn't make me part of the team. I was, indeed, just some school kid who had turned up and thrown himself around a bit. The empty feeling was about as unexpected as any of us can experience. This was supposed to have been the ultimate big day for me. I'd been extremely naïve to think I could have been accepted as a professional footballer after just one training session.

Walking out of Feethams Car Park, I dragged my sober feelings out with me to my mum whom I'd arranged to meet. I could see her waiting in the car just beyond the gates of the football ground by the cricket scoreboard. I moved over slightly to make sure the car coming out slowly behind me could get past without clipping me and turned round out of idle curiosity. I recognized the driver, Dave Hawker, a regular First Team player we had signed from Hull City a couple of years back, and who we had been running round Abbey Road field with an hour ago.

His car had plenty of room as it happened so I started to turn round to continue my exit. In that instant, Dave did something absolutely monumental that I will never forget as long as I live. As he drove past me, he nodded and waved. The bolt of pride hit me fully and squarely in the chest. In that instant, and for that instant only, I was one of them, part of 'The Team'. You see, he acknowledged me, footballer to 'footballer', not footballer to 'fan', not footballer to 'autograph hunter'. For that instant, even if in footballing terms for no other time in my life, I was his equal. In that one moment I knew what it felt like to be a footballer with Darlington FC. I waved back as he sped past and away round the cricket pitch.

Mark Wilson
Prize Winner

Mark Wilson never played professional football. After university, and spells as a rock band manager, a project co-ordinator with BBC Education and an admin officer at a local college, he is now a creative copywriter with a Sunderland based media agency. He still regularly watches Darlington FC – from the East Stand.

The Eastbourne Generation Dancers and Concert Party

The Eastbourne Generation Dancers and Concert Party, formerly Eastbourne Methodist Go-Go Dancers entertained the handicapped, pensioners, hospital patients, nursing home residents, women's institutes and garden parties for nearly twenty-five years. They also raised thousands of pounds for charities.

It all began at the Eastbourne Methodist Youth Club in Yarm Road, Darlington, where regular discos were held. It was noticed that there were some excellent

How it all started! Eastbourne Methodist Youth Club Go-Go Dancers, 1969. They are rather differently dressed from Dancing Fashion in later years!(p. 108) (Copyright, North of England

dancers. Bernie Pentony, Rob Errington, Mike Lodge and Anne Ford decided to put these dancers to good use. After putting their heads together, they picked a few of the girls, raised funds for costumes and from then on took bookings from various organisations.

One problem was transport. The girls' parents were very helpful, taking their cars as far as Harrogate, Middlesbrough, Northallerton and Sedgefield. The group was getting more popular, however, so a fund was started to raise money for a mini-bus. It wasn't long before 100 bookings were reached and it was decided to celebrate the 100th show at The Civic Theatre in Darlington. There was a good audience including Lady Starmer MBE who always supported the group. The evening raised a lot of money for charity and provided a swimming pool for the handicapped.

There were now over fifty girls all doing their best to get into one of the teams. In 1974 the club was selected to represent Darlington at The Royal Albert Hall in the Methodist Association of Youth Clubs' annual show. At this time the choreographer was Anne Ford and she made up a routine to the music of *Hawaii Five-0*. The item involved thirty girls and had to be danced to a live orchestra. A coach-load of girls and supporters enjoyed a great

The dancers practising outside The Royal Albert Hall, 1974.

weekend. The first performance on the afternoon went perfectly, receiving a standing ovation. The local *Evening Despatch* photographed the girls outside The Albert Hall and it was published on the Saturday evening before the second performance. What a thrill for friends, parents and the people of Darlington!

The performance had gone so well that the group was asked to return the following year. This time the item was 'Dancing Through the Ages' and was choreographed by Pauline Bennett. To get the dancing correct old-time dance groups were visited and their help greatly appreciated. The difficult job was finding two lads to take part. However, Peter Lavin and Taffy Davies 'volunteered'. Everything was going well but on the morning of departure Peter had an

enormous gumboil and was in considerable pain. Not wanting to let anyone down, he still travelled and managed to take part.

When we arrived at The Royal Albert Hall I was told that I would have to give instructions to the people working the lights around the arena. I had no idea what to do but a few words from the producer of the show and more good luck than anything else, managed to get the spotlights working at the correct place and time.

The following year Darlington was again asked to dance, this time at the Westminster Hall. The item this year was 'Jesus Christ Superstar', a dance that later became popular in many churches in the area. Our next visit to the capital was to dance at The Victoria Palace Theatre, another fantastic success. The Victoria Palace was home to the *Black and White Minstrel Show* but we were amazed to see the condition of the costumes hanging in the girls' dressing room. They were torn and filthy, nothing like you saw on television.

By now the bookings were coming in quickly. Regular venues were Morris Grange, a holiday home for the handicapped and Winterton Hospital. In December 1990 we completed twenty-eight shows in thirty-one days, even going out on Christmas Eve and Boxing Day. We shall never forget one booking we attended at Winterton Hospital. A patient present at the show had not spoken for over two years. She could communicate only by shaking or nodding her head and the ward sister held her hand throughout the performance. Expecting some sort of head movement, the sister asked 'old Annie' how she had enjoyed the show. 'Old Annie' spoke quite clearly, 'weren't they lovely?' I don't mind admitting that a few of us shed tears and we went from Winterton ten-foot-tall. This made it all worthwhile and never to be forgotten. Many other cases were told of patients who would not walk across a room or move from their seats. At the end of a performance, however, the girls would ask patients to dance with them, and they would dance superbly.

We were always on the look out for new music and costumes but we still did not make a charge for any of our shows. The

A few of the Eastbourne Generation Dancers based at Eastbourne Hall in Cobden Street.

Dancing Fashion, 1994.

Darlington Lions Club came to our aid. They had seen a mini bus for sale so we gave them all the money we had in the bank and they added the remainder. At last we did not have to rely on a parent's kindness. Peter Lavin was our first driver with Pauline Pentony, who was by now also choreographer, standing in. Later, Pauline took over when Peter's job meant he could no longer help us out.

The group now began to concentrate on their charity work and so Eastbourne Generation was formed, along with an older girl team, Dancing Fashion. Representing Darlington these groups won over sixty awards, including a trophy awarded by Durham County Association of Youth clubs to the club who had done the most for the community. They won this award fifteen years in succession.

Dancing Fashion comprised nine girls, all over seventeen years of age. A donation would be asked for their performances in order to help fund the younger teams. Eastbourne Dancers organized another great charity night at the Fiesta Club in Stockton. The dancers were support to Charlie Williams, the comedian and to singers with Bruce Forsyth's daughter.

Plans were made for a twenty-five year celebration but disaster struck. Pauline Pentony, the choreographer had to go into hospital for some time. Although efforts were made to keep going, dancers began slipping away to other groups or just simply lost interest. It is now seven years since Eastbourne Generation and Dancing Fashion folded, yet there are still people making enquiries about their availability. They were twenty-five years I will never forget. Thousands of photographs remind me of the happiness the group brought to both the dancers and the people who attended the performances.

Bernard Pentony

Darlington – Through the Eye of a Needle

Darlington Branch of the Embroiderers' Guild

Embroidery is a quiet skill, often valued for that calming, therapeutic quality it transmits to those who pick up a needle. It is not perceived as an art form with a reputation for scoring a major, strident impact. It has its own vocabulary, its personalities, its critics and its triumphs. Its threads wind their way into domestic, spiritual and artistic areas of life, often without people being aware of the connection. Contemporary embroidery is heir to a tradition that extends back through history whilst today it looks to the future – to exciting developments and the advantages of up to the minute technology. Embroidery is multi-cultural and crosses boundaries and frontiers. The language of needle and thread seldom needs an interpreter and is recognized worldwide for its beauty and character.

The Embroiderers' Guild, with its network of branches, welcomes and represents the wide variety of people for whom embroidery is a rewarding experience

– admirers as well as makers. I first became aware of the Embroiderers' Guild while I was a student in Lincolnshire. Stitching and embroidery had always been a part of my life and when I moved to the North East it was natural for me to turn to the organisation as a way of meeting new people and making friends. The Cleveland Branch in Middlesbrough was my home base at that time; subsequently my family and I moved to Darlington and myself and two friends travelled to Cleveland for monthly meetings. Other stitching friends in Darlington were more reluctant to make this monthly pilgrimage and the idea of establishing a new Darlington Branch of the Guild began to emerge. In the summer of 1979 our small team of enthusiasts worked to distribute publicity for an exploratory meeting, once we had solved the question of a suitable venue. At that time The Arts Centre in Vane Terrace, Darlington, formerly a teacher training college, was becoming established in its new role as an aspiring host venue for the arts, with staff welcoming groups seeking a meeting place. The date for the meeting was set – 22 September 1979 and we were overwhelmed by the response! A promising number of potential members signed up at that initial meeting and Darlington Branch of the Embroiderers' Guild was officially launched.

The Arts Centre has been the base for the group ever since. We outgrew the original meeting room and have moved around this versatile building which has given us space for practical sessions, workshops, storage, exhibitions and social functions. Speakers and visitors have expressed their admiration and envy that we have such a lively and exciting place in which to meet.

During the first ten years we worked hard to build up the membership and bring our activities and enthusiasm to the attention of the people of Darlington and the surrounding area. The format of the programme gave scope for practical Day Schools and Workshops. These ran alongside the regular monthly meetings where invited speakers shared their embroidery experience with members. The programme has always been compiled with an awareness of the needs of all members across a broad spectrum. We have fought an endless battle against the popular misconception that you have to be an expert to join the Embroiderers' Guild, so from the very early days the aim has been to encourage the beginner whilst at the same time stimulating the committed student and the gifted, talented artist. It did not take long before we could sense the social and personal benefits members gained from the embroidery experience and friendships and support were quick to generate.

We built up a library of specialist books for the benefit of members. We organized excursions to spirit members along to embroidery exhibitions and collections further afield and visited the Head Office of the Guild at Hampton Court Palace. We forged links with embroidery requisite suppliers who could provide those vital items which can be difficult to track down.

Whilst the Arts Centre remained our base we spread activities to other locations and benefited from liaison with different centres. Bennett House has always welcomed embroiderers at classes and talks and the Civic Theatre hosted an early exhibition of members' work in the Stalls Bar. St Cuthbert's Church Hall in the Market Square became our venue for ambitious meetings when we encouraged extra visitors and friends to join us for a full one-day meeting. The guest speaker would

be a star attraction from the embroidery galaxy and the accompanying display of embroidery and not least the home-made teas were irresistible. These bumper days were hard work but so rewarding – flushed with success we felt we could tackle anything!

In 1987 Darlington Branch felt ready to open its doors to encourage young embroiderers. The Embroiderers' Guild involved children through the Young Embroiderers Society and individual branches were able to support this initiative through the creation of local groups. Linda Edwards volunteered to spearhead our scheme and assumed the role of group leader, the first step along a long road which demanded great commitment and energy but which kindled and developed an interest in stitching and textiles for a generation of youngsters.

It was not long before our confidence and self-belief were put to the test. The mayor of Darlington, Heather Scott, adopted St Theresa's Hospice as her charity for her year in office and set to work on ideas for a major appeal. She was fired with enthusiasm for creating a stitched panel where all stitches would be sponsored, and she felt that Darlington Embroiderers' Guild members were just the group to make this dream a reality. This was a challenge on a scale previously un-dreamt of but the then chairman, Jaqué Fletcher, gave it 110 per cent support. The committee and members worked hard – on a very short time schedule – to get the whole project up and running. The artistic, practical and logistical problems were formidable but 'Sponsor a Stitch' was launched. For a year the embroidery was displayed at diverse events in and around Darlington. It was seen by thousands of people and admired at craft fairs, shopping malls, Brownie and Guide meetings, summer teas, Christmas markets. members of the public donated and stitched – or donated 'a flower' which represented £10, or requested that their personal fundraising effort should be registered in terms of stitching on the panel. The appeal raised a considerable contribution to the fundraising, of which we were justly proud. The panel was finally completed, framed and presented to the hospice and became a memorial to Jaqué Fletcher who tragically did not live to see its final installation. The panel continues to give pleasure and inspiration to hospice guests, staff and visitors alike.

It is hardly surprising that when we achieved our tenth birthday we felt it was time for a significant celebration. The activities of the first ten years should not be allowed to pass unrecognized. We returned to the well-tried and tested formula of guest speaker, embroidery display, specialist suppliers, good food and excellent company. Our one-day extravaganza, this time at the Dolphin Centre, was a memorable event and many members still retain their commemorative pottery mug or vase as a souvenir.

Darlington Embroiderers' Guild has enjoyed a rewarding relationship with that other, long-standing Darlington 'institution' Coats Crafts UK – formerly Paton & Baldwins. Both the hospice project and the Young Embroiderers (the Young Textile Group as it went on to become) benefited from support. Coats Crafts has always been generous in support for the guild nationally and in particular for the home team in Darlington where the company has given practical help with resources for textile projects in our local area.

The success of the hospice project gave a

Stitched panel for St Theresa's Hospice.

boost to our confidence. The timing might have been preordained as it allowed us to test our strength before the next challenge emerged on the horizon. This took the form of the National Garden Festival at Gateshead in 1990. One of a series of National Garden events around the UK the year long programme beckoned with opportunities for participation by community groups. Always acutely aware that embroiderers need to seek opportunities to showcase their craft, we set about investigating possible ideas and dates. The result was built on successful co-operation between five Guild Branches in the North East: Darlington, Cleveland, Guisborough, Newcastle and Sunderland. The target was an autumn Harvest Festival theme weekend in the Horticultural Hall and the embroiderers took the challenge to heart – creating three-dimensional fruit and vegetables. Stitched cauliflowers, leeks, mushrooms and other vegetables took shape and 'grew' to fill the market stall, which featured at the heart of the display. Small wonder that the exhibit won one of the Festival Awards!

It is easy for the larger, high profile events to overshadow the more intimate displays and exhibitions that over the years have given pleasure to the people of Darlington

Embroiderers' Guild stand, National Garden Festival, Gateshead, 1990.

and communicated the embroidery experience to a wider public. How many people recall the displays in Building Society windows, in the Craft Tent at Darlington Show, at St Mary's church in Gainford or at the Bank Holiday Weekend events at Broken Scar Pumping Station or Bishop Middleham? A chance for visitors to admire the embroidery, pick up information and talk to the demonstrators about the finer points of the current work in progress.

Significant milestones are a wonderful stimulus. When they occur at well-loved centres of our heritage they can be irresistible. In 1992 Darlington Branch was proud to be part of the centenary programme of events at the Bowes Museum in Barnard Castle. An Embroiderers' Day was organized incorporating many of the familiar features but this occasion also afforded the perfect setting in which to include embroidery with historical associations. The Bowes Museum acts as a magnet for embroiderers and since then members have returned repeatedly to recharge the batteries of inspiration and delight. Our 1997 exhibition, Embroiderers at the Bowes, illustrated how the fabric of the building and its treasure store of exhibits can fire the imagination and enliven the creative process.

In 1993 the setting changed to Durham Cathedral for Cathedral 900. An invitation to exhibit within such a magnificent location is a significant honour and Darlington Embroiderers' Guild responded nobly. The event deserved VIP treatment and stimulated the creation of new embroideries as a response to the setting and its associations. The final exhibition was a delight and as rewarding for those who had participated as for the visitors who lingered in the Chapel of the Nine Altars.

In common with many similar organisations, during our time of growth in the town we have felt the ebb and flow of our parent body and responded to changes as they arose. We have been integrated into the Guild Regional structure in the North East and were able to bring this to the forefront of our activities in 1995 when we hosted the North East Regional Day at Darlington Technical College. The region, which at that time stretched from the Scottish borders to mid-Lincolnshire and included all of Yorkshire, sent delegates and the Head Office of the Guild was represented by staff from London. Darlington became the focus for visitors with over 300 attending. The *Northern Echo* and *Darlington and Stockton Times*, ever responsive to our activities, gave comprehensive coverage and excellent publicity.

One of the crowning glories of the Regional Day was the success of a Darlington member, Barbara Clarke, in becoming the winner of a prestigious Guild Award for ecclesiastical embroidery. Awards and competitions are not for everyone but have remained a feature of our programme throughout twenty-one years. They can be a stimulus for positive, persuasive encouragement at all levels. The format of our programme has often become the launch pad for new talent; to convince reticent stitchers that their light should emerge from under its sheltering bushel. Several members have aspired to greater heights and received recognition of their skill at national level.

Darlington Branch has seldom stood still. In the 1990s there never seemed to be time to catch breath – or close the workbox. The 1996 Year of Visual Arts is indelibly printed in our collective consciousness as the year of

'The Needle Points North'. Alongside all visual arts activists we needed to ensure that our art was recognized and celebrated during the year and Northern Arts had tremendous confidence in our ability to deliver. Darlington Branch was one player amongst a large number of branches in the area covered by the programme for the year. This project for the guild regionally, funded by Northern Arts, also presented different challenges, requiring professional/amateur artist partnerships and unfamiliar parameters, pressures and deadlines. The Darlington Panel is a significant statement

Darlington Panel from the series 'The Needle Points North'.

Darlington 2000. Designers with panels before completion, June, 2000.

of the skill and commitment of members. The colourful inner panel represents the visual arts in Darlington and translates these familiar images into fabric and stitch. It proudly took its place beside its fourteen companion panels to represent the town in a successful exhibition. Unexpectedly the exhibition set off and took to the road around the UK and the Darlington panel has become a roving ambassador for the town.

In many ways Arts for Everyone consolidated what the Year of Visual Arts began. Through Lottery funding it provided another avenue through which we could apply for the resources to allow us to extend experience, experiment and explore new avenues. The successful application resulted in the creation of Dramatic Heads in 1998. The collaborative aspect of the project allowed members to build on friendships and share experience with members from

Durham City and Hexham Branches. The inspiration source was generated by Darlington Operatic Company's spring production of *Orpheus in the Underworld* at the Civic Theatre; fulfilling one of the aims of Dramatic Heads; which was to reach new audiences. This was achieved by exhibiting the stunning masks and head-dresses at the theatre during the production run. Not content with 'Orpheus' a further group of members turned their attention to Shakespeare and *The Tempest*. This opened the way for collaboration with The Georgian Theatre at Richmond who exhibited the masks over the summer in their unique theatre setting.

By one of those happy coincidences of fate it became obvious that Darlington Embroiderers' Guild was about to celebrate its twenty-first birthday in the incredible Millennium year of 2000! This was an unmissable opportunity that had to be

Darlington 2000. A Celebration in Stitches. Project co-ordinator, Helen W. Kendrick with the set of seven panels. (Copyright, The Darlington and Stockton Times)

celebrated with style and panache and become a memorable occasion. Ideas were discussed, choices made, decisions taken. Members responded to the idea of creating an embroidery that could be presented to the town as a gift and Darlington 2000, a Celebration In Stitches was conceived. The run up to the project took members back to St Cuthbert's for some very serious fundraising with the aid of the Barclays Bank community scheme. Starting life as an embroidery in book form, 'Darlington in Stitches' evolved into a series of separate panels, each one designed to depict an aspect of life in the community of Darlington at the beginning of the twenty-first century. The panels have each been designed by a different individual and as many members as possible contributed to the stitching. The panels embody all that is best in the medium we love: they illustrate a wide variety of techniques, incorporating traditional skills as well as new,

Darlington 2000 Presentation to mayor of Darlington by Helen W. Kendrick, 30 September 2000.

Members at Darlington Arts Centre. (Copyright, The Northern Echo)

experimental styles. There is a wealth of detail and character and they reach out with direct communication and appeal.

The presentation to the mayor of Darlington, Dorothy Long, took place at the Darlington Branch 21st Birthday event which was held at Polam Hall School on 30 September 2000. Given our long-standing association with Darlington Arts Centre it was appropriate that the panels should first be exhibited in those galleries.

The project has been registered with the National Needlework Record, a register of all needlework created to celebrate the Millennium. The seven embroidered panels are our legacy to the people of Darlington and a fitting heirloom for our contribution to the life of the town.

Our members frequently fit embroidery into busy lives. Their skill is shared in many ways; with families and friends through the stitching of personal and precious gifts – through commissions to enhance our ecclesiastical and formal heritage and traditions – as a means of individual artistic expression for those with creative talents, which often reflect current styles, trends and social influences. As a group we value sharing of skills and generosity of spirit; at meetings there is humour, friendship, opportunity and encouragement. Over its span of twenty-one years Darlington Branch has been enriched through a melting pot of personalities; individuals come and go and influence events. We need to acknowledge the invaluable contribution of a large number of people to the success of the branch. However, we are acutely aware of the need to grow and attract new members and, in common with many organisations, we compete with market forces and rely heavily on voluntary commitment to survive.

Members welcome the opportunities of the future. The Head Office of the organisation is to move to the north – which must be good news for the northern groups. The Guild Centenary is approaching in 2006, another cause for celebrating, for evaluation and anticipating the next phase. As embroiderers we are conscious of our responsibilities for safeguarding our heritage; we also look to the future with optimism and enthusiasm and actively encourage a new generation of embroiderers to discover the rewards and delights that are there for the taking. The next twenty-one years – who knows!

Joy Bradshaw
Founder member, Darlington Embroiderers'
Guild

CHAPTER 6
The Surrounding Area

A family is pictured outside one of the terraced houses near The Emerson Arms, c. 1890.

Historical Hurworth

Hurworth is a pleasant, picturesque village three and a half miles south-east of Darlington. Situated alongside the meandering River Tees and dense woodlands, it is clear how the village acquired its name. Hurworth is translated as 'wood by the water', the word 'hurst' once meaning 'a wood'. The village is home to many quaint Georgian cottages located around The Green. These are in contrast to several Victorian mansions. This unique place is full of interest and

Standing near one of the outhouses to the rear of the terraces.

mystery, as so many houses are situated in secluded places. Hurworth is a magical village with many discovered secrets, yet many mysteries still unturned.

South of Hurworth, is the iron bridge that crosses the River Tees. From here, heading north into the village the Otter and Fish public house is on the right, on a corner of terraced houses. On the opposite side of the road amongst another terraced row is a public house called The Emerson Arms. These terraces were once a hive of industry. The quaint little cottages were home to a thriving community of linen weavers. Born to just a handful of families, the residents would spin stem-fibre from locally grown flax into thread. The peak of the industry was around 1830. Some terraces still feature the windows close to the eaves, which increased light intake for the weavers. It is said that even today, a restless weaver can still be seen working!

The Emerson Arms was named after the famous self-taught mathematician William Emerson. The large arched doorway was once the entrance for the coaches, and the pub's beer garden was once stables. The house opposite the pub

The Emerson Arms. The centre window with the arch was at one time the main entrance, and the large square modern entrance was once the access to the rear stables.

Dover Court situated on The Village Green. The brick building to the left (the garage) is believed to have been the first village school. To the rear is the old bell tower.

also features the archways where the coaches would go through. William Emerson was born in May 1701 at a Georgian house on the Village Green. A sundial mounted on the wall, marks the house of his birth. Various other older houses in the village have sundials designed by William, who was also famous for his books on maths, geometry and navigation.

Following the row of cottages brings you to the grounds of All Saints church. Built on a high bank overlooking the Tees Valley, the church was restored in 1871.

Of the original building, the remains are the western tower and the nave piers, which belong to the Norman Transitional Period. The rest of the restored church includes several periods of Gothic architecture. Directly opposite the church is a three-storey house, painted white. This is believed to have been the old cotton mill of Hurworth.

The main road alongside the church approaches The Village Green, where many magnificent houses are located. There is a house on the left side of The Green called Dover Court. With its castle-style walls it is surely one of the village's most curious buildings. Dover Court has recently had the rendering removed; which uncovered hidden secrets. Once the garage was scraped clean, two arched windows appeared. The arches, along with the building itself, neatly fit the description of the village's first school. Also a bell tower was discovered under many years' growth of ivy. It is believed this is the bell that was struck to warn villagers of plague stricken bodies floating down the river, to be buried under The Green.

In 1665 the year of 'The Great Plague', bodies from nearby villages are reported to have been ferried down the River Tees and brought to Nellgate. This was a narrow passage linking the river to The Green. The bell at Dover Court would have rung to warn villages to go inside their homes. A lone gravedigger would then bury the bodies with lime in mass graves. The lime was filled from storage pits housed in a lime yard next to the Bay Horse public house. This is on the opposite side of the road to The Village Green.

The three hollow dips in the green remain a permanent memorial to the victims of this past tragedy. According to church records, up to 1,500 bodies are submerged under The Green. From a population of 750, Hurworth was left with just 75 residents.

The very large house on The Green is The Old Hall. This huge building was built in the early eighteenth century and was home to the Collyer family. The house and beautiful gardens overlook the river. Another house of interest on The Green is a long, cream building, built in the seventeenth century. This was the Old

Parsonage and its door came from the parish church.

Towards the north of the village near Hurworth Place are two more amazing examples of architecture. The Grange, built around 1875, was a wedding gift from Alfred Backhouse, the famous Quaker banker, to his nephew James Backhouse. It was designed by Alfred Waterhouse. Today, this is Hurworth Community Centre.

The second old building in the north of the village is Rockcliffe House. This house is on the opposite side of the road to The Grange and down a long sheltered driveway. Built in 1863 it was first owned by Alfred Backhouse. The house has a beautiful stained glass window, and underground tunnel system.

Further north down the main road there is another row of interesting terraced houses on Hurworth Road. Once known as Station Terrace, the houses were built in the 1890s. Several members of the Backhouse family once owned Hurcroft House, a hotel situated amongst the terrace, which was a row of shops. Across the railway bridge from here and down a steep bank, is Croft Bridge, where the River Tees separates County Durham from North Yorkshire.

Hurworth is a magical village, home to many families and interesting characters. The buildings are all unique, holding their own secrets.

Zoë Hadrick

Memories Of Cockerton

One of the attractive areas of Darlington is the former village of Cockerton which lost

A photograph taken by Mr Hodgson-Brown of the straw bonnet maker of Cockerton, Mr W. Mounsey.

NEGATIVES KEPT.

Straw Bonnet Maker

Hodgson-Brown,
Photographer,
5, ÷ ASTON ÷ TERRACE,
Cockerton,
Darlington.

FURTHER COPIES OR ENLARGEMENTS MAY BE
OBTAINED AT ANY TIME.

Mr Hodgson-Brown was a local photographer who lived in Aston Terrace, Cockerton.

its rural status in 1915. Despite recent modern buildings it still retains many characteristics of a village; a good example of which is its spacious tree-lined village green. Many years ago it formed part of the Saxon Mark and comprised some four and a half acres. For centuries the copyholders were allowed to graze their geese and donkeys.

Cockerton is an ancient village and its name is derived from the Saxon *kukrus* or winding stream. The small Saxon settlement was called *Kukroston* which was changed through the years to Cockerton.

In the summer the green is often used for church and scout fêtes and is enhanced by a large fountain, no longer working, but used to display plants and flowers. It is overlooked by St Mary's church, the Holy Family Roman Catholic church and the Methodist chapel.

One of the most respected residents, Miss Hilda Scarr, whose house overlooks the green, is the daughter of the late Mr R. Scarr. He was highly regarded as a local historian and for many years was the organist at the Methodist chapel.

One of the lesser-known aspects of Cockerton, but highly interesting, is a terrace of five Victorian houses known as Aston terrace. The terrace nestles behind the Methodist chapel. One of the early occupants of No. 3 Aston Terrace was Mr Hodgson-Brown, a local photographer.

Aston Terrace was built by Mr Greener, who named the terrace after his estate in Aston Flintshire. In 1873 Mr Greener tried to get a seat on Darlington Town Council but was defeated by T. Monell by six votes. Mr Greener also wanted to straighten the River Skerne. It is interesting to note that Mr R. Scarr wrote in 1952, 'If this advice had been acted on at the time the town would have been spared the seemingly endless trouble resulting from polluted conditions of our local "Tiber".'

Mr Greener became a mining engineer and a coal agent. He made much money during the Franco-German war; in addition to all his business interests he gave great service to Cockerton Methodism. He became the treasurer of the church building scheme in 1872, a leading spirit he also took classes.

His association with the leading industrialists of the district enabled him to procure a generous flow of subscriptions for the new work. Perhaps Mr Greener's greatest claim to fame came in March

1873 when he had the responsible position of chairman of the jury, which condemned Mary Ann Cotton, the West Auckland poisoner, to death.

Two years after Cockerton Methodist chapel was built Thomas Greener suffered severe business losses and left the district.

Those acquainted with the records of the time will know that it is to his cultured and aesthetic qualities in collaboration with Ross and Lamb architects that the residents of Cockerton have a fine Methodist chapel and a little known terrace of houses.

Kate Vokes

Yare's Old Antique Shop, High Northgate. (Copyright, Centre for Local Studies, Darlington Library)

Alex Martino selling ice cream on the corner of Vane Terrace/Abbey Road, 1940s. (Copright, Centre for Local Studies, Darlington Library)

An Old Fashioned Wedding
A Poem by Ron Watson

O' Aycliffe, ancient village, where did you
get your name?
We must dust the withered leaves from of
your oaken frame.
For an oaken forest once you were, the
acorn was your crown,
Who could guess from this beginning, the
emergence of a town?

The Oak and acorn then was *Acle*, then
Yackley you became,
A Saxon cross within your church denotes
your claim to fame.

The first 'Synod' on England's soil was held beneath your trees,
Where men of God brought Christian faith and fell upon their knees.
Your forests now have long since gone, you
have felt the wind of change.
A new town now surrounds you and it must seem very strange,
To have lost your trees to factories, plastic, steel and brick,
As progress marches on my friend it would
seem a cruel trick.

But Newton Aycliffe will remember you and
all your long lost charms,
For your history is depicted on your new
town's coat of arms.

Now the Saxon village of Yoden has a
hidden history,
Was it built to warn the Saxons of raiders from the sea?
Or did the people living there while in their daily toil,
Find something hard and shining black beneath that Durham soil?

But coal it was and coal they found, beneath that sparse and barren ground,
And from that time they slogged and tore, in sickness and in health,
To invest against the future with this hard earned new found wealth.
But the man who knew the heartache of the men who won the coal,
Of the difference between poverty, and hunger and the dole,
Who fought their rights and arguments, all miners will agree,
This shining lamp for pitmen was a man called Peter Lee.

But now the pits are dying and they need new industry,
So they built a brand new town there and they called it Peterlee.
Now Peterlee and Aycliffe are some twenty miles apart,
And a lot of people spoke about these towns without a heart,
But heart they have, and heart they've shown, not like sister or like brother,
But they have a similar purpose, so they've grown to love each other.
Now the councillors and dignitaries who have helped to forge this link,
Are very wise and practical and are now upon the brink,
Of joining them together, to make them man and wife,
Let's hope they prosper as of old, to an even longer life.

Acknowledgements

Ottakar's is grateful to everyone who has made publication of this book possible. Firstly, *Radio Cleveland*, *The Northern Echo* and all those who, in the early stages, publicszed the writing competition. Thanks go to all those who entered the competition and made compiling the book such an enjoyable experience. Thanks also to Ron Watson, Derek Wellburn, Janet Hossell, Keith Bulman, Stephen Collins, J. Copland, Gordon Coates, and P. Oliver who all generously lent or gave permission for photographs or postcards to be used in the final publication. A special mention to the staff of The Centre for Local Studies at Darlington Library who patiently helped in the hunt for photographs and in giving permission for those from their own stock to be used. Finally, enormous thanks must go to *The Northern Echo*, especially Chris Lloyd, the assistant editor and writer of the 'Echo Memories' column. Not only did Chris search for photographs to be included but he also took on the unenviable task of choosing the three prize-winning articles.